MW01071501

Nicolaitan

Lords of Hypocrisy

Bruce S. Bertram

Acts 20:26–27 ESV. Therefore I testify to you this day that I am innocent of the blood of all, for I did not shrink from declaring to you the whole counsel of God.

Nicolaitan
Lords of Hypocrisy

Published by
The Word of God Ministries

www.wholebible.com
YouTube channel: The Whole Bible Christian

ISBN 978-0-9975014-2-1

Printed in the United States of America

Many thanks to my wife of almost 40 years for helping to edit my work, and provide (or attempt to provide) all sorts of good comments improving the text. She has encouraged me in so many ways when it felt like the world was against me. I know why Adam shared the fruit offered by Eve.

This book is not for the average churchgoer who thinks everything is fine in the Church, or even just their church. This is for the people who are aware that something is not right in the Church and wonder why. It's for those who hunger and thirst for God and can't understand why they seem to be starving.

1 Discovery

Job 36:22, ESV. Behold, God is exalted in his power; who is a teacher like him?

On his last visit to Ephesus, Paul warns the congregation leaders about the future appearance of bad shepherds coming from within the congregation.

Acts 20:29–30, ESV. I know that after my departure fierce wolves will come in among you, not sparing the flock; and from among your own selves will arise men speaking twisted things, to draw away the disciples after them.

About 30 years after this, Jesus warns the Ephesians (and Pergamum) about Nicolaitans in Revelation chapter two. Obviously, Nicolaitans were some of those wolves about which Paul warned. Did the wolves disappear after John wrote the Revelation, or have they survived to populate modern congregations? Did believers get rid of false teachers, or have they spread out from Ephesus and Pergamum in the last 2,000 years and continue to speak "twisted things?" The Church identifies wolves as those who don't follow "orthodox" Church teachings. But what if those making that judgment are Nicolaitans in sheep's clothing? Could the "orthodox" teachings be unbiblical? How do we tell?

Jesus mentions the Nicolaitans in two of the letters He dictated to the seven congregations in Revelation 2 and 3. Their origin and exact teachings are not clear, but He groups them with other false teachers and those whose works He hates. This is important because Nicolaitans are, in fact, still around; just with different names. They might only be mentioned a couple of times in the Bible, but they have indeed spread throughout the Church/synagogue and have a lot of influence.

We need to understand their works and why Jesus hates those works, because they are causing a lot of harm and directing people away from God's Word. In this book I'm going to show that not only were Nicolaitans a problem in 95 A.D. when John wrote the book of Revelation, but have always been a problem. In the next chapter, I'll define them from the Bible. Then I'll define them by fruit, how they teach and what they teach. I offer further evidence for my case from history, and a comparison of the Bible with modern Church teachings.

One of the major tactics of people who want to hide truth is to change names and redefine words. Nicolaitans use different labels, and they all claim to be shepherds now, not wolves. Using labels such as shepherd disguises what they really are and what they are doing to the flock. The problem with that is the Bible also tells us about bad shepherds, and the descriptions match. They don't call themselves Nicolaitans, but wolves or bad shepherds are all over the place. I'll connect the dots and show their works, so believers realize who they are, avoid them, and turn to the Bible.

I could write this book two ways. One is the nice, sweet approach where I dance around the issues and try not to hurt feelings. The other way is to be blunt, and if I step on some toes so be it. I chose the blunt way for two reasons. The first is that Nicolaitans rob us of maturity, fruit of the Spirit and abundant life, and do a lot of other bad things too as Jesus says in Matthew 23. The second reason is the sweet way just doesn't work to rescue people from Nicolaitan teachings; hearts are hard and the Nicolaitans fight tooth and nail to defend their turf and their money. Jesus, Paul, Peter, Jude, Jeremiah, Ezekiel and others chose the blunt way, so I'm in good company.

I am a whole Bible Christian. I believe that the entire Bible, including The Law, Torah or the Law of Moses, is necessary in the believer's life - in contrast to those who teach most Christians that the Law is "fulfilled" and hence mostly eliminated. The entire Bible is filled with living oracles full of the love of Jesus, given to believers for discipleship and without error in what it teaches. The word Torah means instruction, and all of His Words instruct believers in how to live. My family follows God's instructions such as those for holidays, diet, and Sabbath. We've seen, through the simple reading of His Word, that Jesus did not eliminate the Law. He gave it to Moses, lived it, taught it, and confirmed it to His followers. More about "whole Bible living" is in my book <u>Whole Bible Christianity, Blessings Pressed Down and Overflowing</u>.

Whole Bible Christians believe that much of what God says of Himself, and what He requires of man, can be understood from simply reading and doing the Bible. The whole Book; not just our favorite 16 verses or Paul's letters. We also resist the tendency to only follow what we hear others say about the Bible, and read it ourselves. So I'm one of those the Church calls a false teacher. But am I false compared to the Bible, or compared to Church "orthodoxy" that may not be biblical? Find out in this book.

Jesus had a problem with Jewish bad shepherds because they grabbed authority but wrongly interpreted the Law and the Prophets. They made inaccurate rulings from the Law and sought earnestly for ways to implement more of their man-made laws. Many Jews regard these rulings and interpretations, called "oral law" or Mishnah, as on the same level as, (though they frequently override) the written Word. I'll show you that modern Nicolaitans have done the same thing for the Church. Church leaders too have developed a lot of "oral law;" interpretation and traditions that mostly override the Bible.

I arrived at the understanding that the whole Bible is a God-given lifestyle and discipleship method for all believers through a lot of searching and painful loss. It was sort of like wandering in the desert as I experienced fifteen Churches in ten different denominations by the time I was 40. These were Churches where I stayed for a while, not just visited a few times. I was baptized a Catholic and did the catechism and first Holy Communion thing early on. I was there in the '60's when "folk masses" first began to percolate and Vatican II was wrapping up. Assembly of God, Methodist, and Baptist were next. After getting married, we went to Calvary Chapel for three years. Then there was the Presbyterian, Wesleyan, another Calvary Chapel, an Evangelical Free, a Bible Church, and some Messianic synagogues, which turned out to be the Church in a prayer shawl.

In my extensive experiences with different Church governments and leaders, I saw a variety of approaches to Bible teaching and problem solving. That, along with decades of questions, self-teaching, some seminary classes and Bible study, gives me insight on the Nicolaitan issue. I also come at it from once upon a time being a Nicolaitan. Yep. I learned from them, and for a long while taught the same things in the same ways. But I kept trying to learn more and connect with Jesus better.

Around 1997 I made some big changes as I started to figure out that the whole Bible, Genesis to Revelation, was for all believers to follow. A believing Jewish friend helped by pointing out Bible teachings that are hijacked by non-believers. Problems arose when I tried to share the things I was learning with friends and leaders. They told me in many ways why I was wrong. Except they couldn't show me from the Bible; they had to resort to "orthodox" Church doctrine.

When I first began to read through the whole Bible and learn the principles of whole Bible Christianity, I was explaining some of it to a Nicolaitan. He asked if I thought I was a prophet, and if so what was my message. I was surprised by the questions, but it only took two seconds of thought to say my message was, "Repent." I told him I don't think I'm a prophet in the class of, say, Isaiah or Jeremiah, but anyone who speaks God's Word is, in a sense, a prophet. Prophets have at least two functions. To "forth-tell" the Word so people repent, and to "foretell" what would happen if they didn't. All of us who live and speak God's living oracles are "forth telling" prophets or teachers. The message is not ours, but God's.

I continued to sort through my Nicolaitan brainwashing on my own, eliminating the wrong things and plugging in the "new" good things I was learning from the practice of the whole Word. Excellent teachers such as Tim Hegg and others from Torah Resource (on the web at www.torahresource.com) provided critical help. It was tough shedding my Nicolaitan thought processes contrary to the Word. It was also hard losing my Nicolaitan friends. I would rather they had seen the truth and repented.

On the upside, I had no position with a paycheck, so I didn't have to worry about losing income. I did lose a position as an unpaid elder and another as an unpaid youth leader (for teaching the truth), though. That's a problem for a lot of Nicolaitans: changing to biblical teaching will cost them everything. They risk it all if they start teaching the Bible instead of standard Church doctrine. Either the congregation slaps them down or the denomination will. Calvary Chapel calls it "losing your dove." In that Church, you can't teach anything other than what is approved by Chuck Smith (may he rest in peace) and his disciples. If you do, then like a franchise they will make you give up the dove symbol and the name. The home office controls what you teach and how you sell it. Stray from their guidelines and you're out of business.

All franchises, er, Churches, have ways to control heresy and heretics. To the Church bureaucracy, a heretic is one who departs from "orthodox" teachings. Orthodox means accepted. Accepted means that a bunch of "experts" got together and decided what was right. Of course, the Church swamp dwellers want you to think that "orthodox" also means "biblical," but in many ways, their dogma is not. Stick with the home office orthodoxy and your job is safe. Step outside of that and the paychecks disappear. They will call you a "cult," which the dictionary says is "a religion regarded as unorthodox or spurious." They overlook the fact that compared to Acts 2 all modern Churches fall into that category. On the one hand, the orthodox systems are there for a good reason; they keep nutcases from messing up the franchise. On the other hand, the systems frequently turn into self-perpetuating, hardened, bomb-proof bunkers that are almost impossible to change if they are wrong. It's not just a "liberal" or "conservative" or "evangelical" thing either. It's all through the Church.

What I hope for you with the writing of this book is to help you establish a better connection to God, show the truth in the Word, encourage you with life more abundant and assist you to become more mature (Hebrews 5:11-6:3). Modern Nicolaitans and their bureaucracies (the word means "rule by desk") are misdirecting us and robbing us of life and freedom in Him. They have placed themselves in our way, offering a pseudo-relationship with an empty caricature of a Jesus and a false hope in a corrupted new covenant. You have a direct relationship with God and don't need any intermediary other than our High Priest Jesus. He tore the curtain in the Temple and is giving us the bread of heaven in the whole of His loving Word. Take it and eat. Circumcise your heart. Ignore the philosophies of men and go right to the source of life.

If I told you there was gold buried in your back yard, and you "believed" me, what would happen next? You wouldn't stop digging till you found it. That's the difference between people who say they believe Jesus, and those who really do. If you "believe" but don't dig, do you really believe?

When I question Nicolaitan teachings, I get all sorts of defenses. The backstop response is, "That's the way we do things here. If you aren't being ministered to, then find a place where you are." This is the polite version of, "If you don't like it, leave."

Almost all churches say this when questioned, because they don't want their kingdoms to fall apart. So I left the Church. But I didn't leave God or His Word. I have found a place where I can receive ministering directly from Jesus without interference. God and His Word are my Minister, my Teacher, and my life.

2 Lords of the Flock

2 Timothy 4:3–4, ESV. For the time is coming when people will not endure sound teaching, but having itching ears they will accumulate for themselves teachers to suit their own passions, and will turn away from listening to the truth and wander off into myths.

As I said before, there are only two places in the Bible that mention Nicolaitans by name, both in Revelation chapter 2. That doesn't mean, though, it's the only place they are found. As I'll show, they are all through the Bible such as in Jeremiah 25:34-36. Nicolaitans made their homes in the cities of Pergamum and Ephesus, but they didn't stay there. There is also a person named Nicolaus in Acts 6 who might be the founder of the Nicolaitans.

We don't know much specifically about the ancient Nicolaitans, like who they are and where they came from. But I find it difficult to believe Jesus would mention them in letters meant for all believers (Revelation 2:7, 11, 17, 29; 3:6, 13, 22) if they were just a local, limited group of teachers. Their works are the important thing according to Jesus, because we know He hates them (Revelation 2:6). We also know that Nicolaitans were neighbors of teachers that taught like Balaam, and that right-thinking Ephesians hated their works. This evidence points to the Nicolaitans simply being a type of false or bad shepherd, like Jezebel or Balaam and many Pharisees.

Pergamum was the place where Satan had his throne (Revelation 2:13), so it makes sense it was a hot spot for false teaching. We know Satan tempts teachers like Balaam to the wrong path by offering them the kingdoms of the world as he did with Jesus. So it's no wonder there were so many false teachers around Pergamum. I think of it like selling franchises. "Such a deal do we have for you. No down payment." But the fine print says it will cost you your soul. A neighbor of the Nicolaitans just down the road in Thyatira bought one franchise. Jesus called her Jezebel, and she taught just like the Balaam teachers. It's important to note that she claimed to be a prophetess, because many Nicolaitans use a position of authority to add weight to their false teachings. It was only a matter of time till the Nicolaitans branched out and would have franchises all over the world as I'm alleging today.

Birds of a Feather. Balaam was a seer who sold his talents to the king of Moab for an attempted cursing of Israel (Numbers 22-24, Joshua 13:22, 2 Peter 2). He ignored God's warnings, including one from a talking donkey, not to do it, because money was a prime motivation for him. Like the donkey, God caused Balaam to talk in a way that blessed Israel instead of cursing. Later, Balaam taught the Midianites to subvert Israel by providing beautiful escorts to some of the men, and who then led them into idolatry. He met his end when Israel killed the kings of Midian (Numbers 31:8). Money is also a prime motivator for many modern Nicolaitans. The prosperity doctrine, which is the teaching that all you need is more of some mysterious "faith" to have wealth and health, is one proof of that. Sexual immorality sweetens the pot and its all part of "if it feels good, do it."

Jezebel was the daughter of Ethbaal king of the Sidonians, wife of Ahab, who was king of the northern ten tribes of Israel (1 Kings 16, 18, 19 and 21; 2 Kings 9). Together these two "did more to provoke the Lord, the God of Israel, to anger than all the kings of Israel who were before" them (1 Kings 16:31-32). Among her many sins she killed the prophets of the Lord (1 Kings 18:4), was challenged by Elijah at Mount Carmel and lost, then threatened him with death. She had Naboth killed so she could give his vineyard to Ahab (1 Kings 21), and promoted Baal worship with prostitution and all sorts of sexual immorality. She also met her end in a violent fashion (2 Kings 9:30-37), just as Elijah (1 Kings 21:20) and Elisha (2 Kings 9:10) prophesied.

The person Jesus calls Jezebel in Revelation was a chip off the old Jezebel's block. Claiming "prophetess" (instead of queen) status was a way of grabbing authority for her false teachings. In similar ways, we Nicolaitans today make false claims of authority and push many anti-biblical teachings. The fruit of all bad shepherds is the same, no matter the name. Ancient Nicolaitans were birds of a feather with Balaam and Jezebel. "So also you have some who hold the teaching of the Nicolaitans" as Jesus says.

> Revelation 2:14–15, ESV. But I have a few things against you: you have some there who hold the teaching of Balaam, who taught Balak to put a stumbling block before the sons of Israel, so that they might eat food sacrificed to idols and practice sexual immorality. So also you have some who hold the teaching of the Nicolaitans.

What's in a name. I suggest we can shine more light on the hated Nicolaitan teachings by looking at the meaning of the name. I'm not a fan of making big doctrines out of a single word, but along with the other evidence I'll present this might be a valid indicator of their works. Many times in Scripture, names and symbols illustrate the nature of people or kingdoms. Nicolaites (Nik-o-lah-ee-tace) in Revelation 2:6 and 15 (Νικολαΐτης Strong's 3531) has a meaning of "victory over, or destruction of, lay people." The way the word is used in the letters to Ephesus and Pergamum, and its associations with hated works and sexual immorality, makes me think the meanings of "destruction of, or victory over lay people" apply to their works.

Another way to refer to the "destruction of" or "victory over lay people" is to call it "domineering" or "dominion" or even "lord it over." Peter encourages leaders to avoid domineering (1 Peter 5:3), and Paul says he doesn't want to "lord it over your faith" (2 Corinthians 1:24). The Pharisees are an example of lording it over the flock. It seems plain that Nicolaitans were another. A shepherd doesn't need a name like Nicolaus to lord it over others. Everyone can do it. Just look around. There are all sorts of leaders in the Church that "lord it over" lay people. Even lay people do it.

It's possible that the Nicolaitans were followers of Nicolaus from Acts 6. He might have started the Nicolaitan teachings in the Church that Jesus said he hates. Nicolaus was one of the original seven deacons picked by the congregation to help the apostles with distributing money to those who needed it. So maybe he started out good, but perhaps he detoured into hated teachings later on. It happens more frequently in the Church than we'd like that leaders start out good and then gradually slide away from the Word. We just don't know about him, and I think it's too much of a stretch to say Nicolaus was the leader of the Nicolaitans. But he could've been. Besides, there are lots of leaders unmotivated by the truth. In Paul's day, many would jump into hated false teachings.

> Philippians 1:15–17, ESV. Some indeed preach Christ from envy and rivalry, but others from good will. The latter do it out of love, knowing that I am put here for the defense of the gospel. The former proclaim Christ out of selfish ambition, not sincerely but thinking to afflict me in my imprisonment.

Bad Shepherds. Nicolaitans are part of a group of six "bad shepherds" mentioned in the seven letters of Revelation: Nicolaitans, teachers of "deep things of Satan," Balaam, Jezebel, Satan and the synagogue of Satan (specifically in Philadelphia) which was composed of those "who say they are Jews and are not, but lie." These are, of course, in addition to the people in those congregations that were going astray and needed to repent. The congregations were loaded with people who were "flocking after" bad shepherds. Bad shepherds are described all throughout the prophets, such as Jeremiah 23, 25 and 50, and Ezekiel 34. We know them by their fruits. What I'm saying is that Nicolaitans belong in the same group as all false teachers or bad shepherds. These six types of bad shepherds have always been around in various forms, and are still around today. "Lords of the flock" (Jeremiah 25:34-35) are in charge, but are not feeding God's sheep with the Word. Names change but the false teachings keep going.

Nicolaitans are a separate group, so maybe they had unique teaching methods that were different from the other bad shepherds. But they were still bad shepherds. Jesus hates the teachings of the Nicolaitans, and He wasn't fond of Balaam, Jezebel and the Pharisees either. So we can place all of them in the category of bad shepherds. All teaching methods leading away from the Word of God are bad, whatever name we want to call the shepherds.

Hated Works. Other places in the Word can perhaps inform us as to the nature of the hated Nicolaitan works (and all bad shepherds). For instance, Matthew 23 has a thorough description of the works of the scribes and Pharisees. It does not look from that chapter that Jesus was thinking of the Pharisees warmly, except for maybe the whole "sentenced to hell" thing in verse 33. The book of Jude also gives us an insight into those who "pervert the grace of our God into sensuality and deny our only Master and Lord, Jesus Christ." In the next chapter, we'll look at Paul's warnings concerning false teachers in places such as 1 Timothy 1:1-11, Ephesians, and Colossians 2.

We can also gather a few things about the Nicolaitans by comparing "hate the works" with what else the Bible says about the things Jesus hates.

> Proverbs 6:16–19, ESV. There are six things that the LORD hates, seven that are an abomination to him: haughty eyes, a lying tongue, and hands that shed innocent blood, a heart that devises wicked plans, feet that make haste to run to evil, a false witness who breathes out lies, and one who sows discord among brothers. (See also Zechariah 8:16–17)

The works of the Nicolaitans that Jesus hates are probably the same types of things spoken of in the Proverbs (and Zechariah's) passage. "A false witness who breathes out lies" goes right along with haughty eyes and a lying tongue when we talk about lording it over others. In fact, all these hated things are marks of domineering. The Nicolaitans, whatever their actual identity, can surely be placed in the categories of "hated" and "false." Just because their methods might be different, it doesn't mean they are different from any others who elevate philosophies of men over the Word of God.

It's important to realize that the Nicolaitans were part of the congregations. They were leaders claiming to teach the Word and follow Jesus, but their works showed them to be liars and false shepherds. Believers in Ephesus hated the works of the Nicolaitans as did Jesus, but in Pergamum the Nicolaitans found some acceptance and agreement. Jesus groups the Nicolaitans together with Balaam and Jezebel, even though the Nicolaitans may have used slightly different methods.

I connect education (sometimes with wealth) with domineering, because frequently the educated lord it over those less so. Education can be in formal schooling but not always. Any sort of training carries with it the possibility of corruption leading to pride and misuse of power. This doesn't mean education is bad; I think leaders should be educated. But they need to be educated in living the whole of the Word and be on guard against pride.

Jewish Nicolaitans/Gentile Pharisees. There's a good chance that Nicolaitans are the Gentile version of the Pharisees. Both have works that Jesus hates. The hated works of the Pharisees came from hypocrisy, which is teaching one thing but not doing what they taught. Pharisees assumed the authority to teach Israel because they "knew better," meaning they understood the Law and the Prophets and claimed to speak for God. Jesus disagreed, because they set aside the commands of God in favor of their traditional rulings, and they didn't actually do what they taught. If they had embraced understanding of the Word and followed it, they would not have allowed merchants onto the Temple grounds, women and Gentiles would not have had separate Temple courtyards, and they would've answered questions from Jesus with wisdom. Humility and a servant's heart would have marked them. In fact, they would've evangelized the world as God intended.

If Jesus was teaching the elimination of the Law, then the Pharisees were right to have Him crucified. The Scriptures cannot be broken (John 10:35). But because they were teaching and doing wrong, and Jesus was teaching and doing right, they had to figure out a sneaky way to get rid of Jesus. If the Pharisees were correctly teaching the Bible, and Jesus was eliminating the Old Testament, then why get so mad at them? Wouldn't Jesus just tell them that you don't have to teach it now because I came to start a new thing?

The fact is Jesus was angry with the Pharisees because they seated themselves in Moses' seat and did NOT purely teach what we call the Old Testament (Matthew 23:1-3). Instead they taught their interpretations and traditions, which had covered over or eliminated much of what Jesus gave at Mt. Sinai. Pharisees were like modern teachers, "preaching but not doing" (Matthew 23:3-4), perhaps touching on the Word sometimes, but re-explaining it in favor of their oral law. They did deeds for public accolades or money, and shut the kingdom of heaven in people's faces while not entering themselves. They twisted the "living oracles" as Stephen called the Law (Acts 7:38) into something that caused people to despair of ever being able to touch God. If this doesn't sound like the bulk of Church teaching, go back and read it again.

Jesus hates the works of both Pharisees and Nicolaitans because each is teaching falsely, albeit in different ways perhaps. Jesus hates any teaching that causes people to detour from God's living oracles.

Jesus tells us to beware of the leaven of the Pharisees in Luke 12:1. Their leaven, which is the same as the leaven of all false teachers including the Nicolaitans, is that they live life differently than their teaching. They are play actors, acting as if they believe God. On the outside, they look holy, but on the inside, they are rotten. They use parts of the Law of Moses in their public teachings, but in their rulings and lives, they don't practice all of it. They accept deferential treatment, the best seats at corporate gatherings, dress differently for instant recognition, and love the title of "shepherd," "rabbi," "priest" or "master." All false teachers earn God's wrath because they assign themselves to speak for God, yet misrepresent Him at most every turn.

Hypocrites are variously defined in the Word as "men of falsehood," "dissemblers" and "vain persons" (Psalm 26:4 ESV and AV), "godless" (Job 36:13, Proverbs 11:9 and others, ESV), "evil doer" (Isaiah 9:17 ESV and AV), and "profane mockers" in Psalm 35:16 ESV. Not a great group in which to be included. Jesus had a lot to say about hypocrites recorded for us in various places, and He applied Isaiah 29:13 in Mark 7:6 ESV to them. "This people honors me with their lips, but their hearts are far from me; in vain do they worship me, teaching as doctrines the commandments of men." We can see that there is not much difference between the doctrines of all false teachers; just a difference in looks. Different wool clothing, if you will.

Modern Nicolaitans reject the Pharisees by name but simply continue with different hated works. They sit in judgment on the Law of Moses, arrogantly sending parts of it to the trash heap and replacing it with their own oral law. They too set aside the commands of God for the sake of their tradition (Matthew 15:3, 6). For instance, there is an emphasis on "the Sabbath" in the creeds and faith statements of most Churches. But even ignoring the fact that their Sabbath is on the wrong day, they still do not behave on Sunday as the Bible says to behave on a Sabbath.

Nicolaitan Marketing. I don't think the Nicolaitans just came out of nowhere just before John wrote Revelation. They were there all along, developing their teachings because of rejection by the world and by the Jewish leaders. Their teachings developed slowly in stages among first, second and third century believers. A little error was introduced ever so gently over the years. By the time a Roman emperor officially recognized the Church in 325 A.D., the false teaching exploded into an art form. It's a very brilliant marketing strategy from the deceiver. Obviously, when John wrote the Revelation, Nicolaitan marketing had born fruit.

A series of events helped the Nicolaitan teaching along. The Temple was destroyed in 70 A.D. When the Temple was gone there were taxes levied on the Jews, which included those believers who looked like Jews because they practiced the Law. Jerusalem was destroyed in 135 A.D. The New Testament writings were collected and called the "New Covenant" at about 200 A.D. So over 150 years, believers went from a Jewish Messiah and Apostles in Jewish synagogues, to a new Gentile "Church" and a "new" covenant which replaced Israel and the "old" covenant.

It looked like God rejected the Jews for the crucifixion, and the Nicolaitans, I think, took advantage of it. The "new" teachings bore very little resemblance to the Olive Tree or biblical new covenant of Jeremiah 31:31-34. But once the Nicolaitans created the new things, it was easy to continue the separation between Israel and the Church. Each of the tragedies boosted the replacement theories. Eventually they added the false "Christ killer" nametag to all those who rejected their new teachings.

The reason I'm taking time to describe the marketing strategy of the Nicolaitans is because the modern Church continues the strategy without letup. Andy Stanley for instance is one of many Nicolaitans who says "Jesus came to launch something new."[1] When he and others like him say "new," they misuse the word to mean something that didn't exist before. They don't mean "renewed" or "refreshed," like a new moon. This is the actual meaning of the word new in "new covenant."

Modern Church Nicolaitans continue to claim that the Old Testament doesn't apply anymore, except as "historical context and inspiration," as Andy Stanley puts it. This dismissal is one of the reasons Jezebel and Balaam types of immorality flourish in churches. When they steer people away from the plain teaching of

---

[1] From an email "This One Might Surprise You," part of "Things someone should've told you when you got your first Bible," from Andy Stanley's Deep

God's living oracles, these sins find a foothold in congregations, and grow with fertilizer from the philosophies of men.

The anti-biblical "new body/new covenant" that Nicolaitans teach is cobbled together from a hodge-podge of cherry-picked verses gleaned from the epistles and the gospels, mixed with elementary principles of the world (Galatians 4:3, 9). They use the result to excuse all sorts of behavior never condoned by God. In fact, all of the Frankenstein-looking "new" teachings resemble many, many old teachings from paganism. They're just dressed up with a few well-chosen Bible verses yanked out of context and given a "new" meaning not intended by the Bible authors. Gentiles are not any more immune to paganism and idolatry than Israel.

Frank Viola is a Nicolaitan who is <u>Reimagining Church</u> (a title of one of his books). But his heart of stone limits his "re-imagining." Reading through his books and articles, one gets the strong impression that his "new" approach is really a rehash of old stuff from "elemental spirits of the world" (Colossians 2:8). He has a good desire for the Church to change, but he wants to do it by mysticism and sentiment instead of a return to God's Word. Mr. Viola regurgitates mystical paganism spouted by many false teachers of the past like Watchman Nee or Marcion. Modern Nicolaitan leaders love to repackage old concepts. That way they can look fresh and new and exciting without doing anything new, such as reimagining church by the Word of God.

Another case in point is from Bill Perkins of Compass International. He holds regular conferences he calls Steeling the Mind. There's usually a group of decent speakers, and they cover subjects related to prophecy, creationism, and current events. I've been to a couple of his conferences and I like them in general, though they come up short in the Scripture department. They are nice people, but the subjects get repetitious and come from a particular dispensational slant. He needs some fresh, biblical blood from Jesus. So I sent him an email with links to our material volunteering my services for speaking. He replied that "I didn't see anything that immediately jumped out that would fit our upcoming conferences." Very nice, very polite. It seemed obvious to me, however, that the material in our book Whole Bible Christianity would be perfect for Steeling the Mind.

I get articles from Compass occasionally and they really leave me wanting more and better Scripture than they provide. In an article titled, "Tying Tassels to Truth" Bill comes close to the truth, but like a lot of Nicolaitans veers away at the last minute back into regular Church dogma. For instance, I extracted this typical Nicolaitan quote from the article.

> "Only a few Jews become Believers in the Church Age. And most of those who do struggle with getting away from the Law. They tend to want to work Jesus into the Law instead of making Jesus' and Paul's instructions their life's focus."

You see that first he says there's some sort of "Church age" which is nowhere in the Bible. The next thing he says is "Jews...struggle with getting away from the Law." Why do they need to get away from the Law? There isn't any Scriptural evidence that would support the idea of "getting away from the Law." It's okay if believers want to stay with God's Law. The Nicolaitan Church has a problem with the Law, not true believers.

The third thing he says is the believing Jews "tend to want to work Jesus into the Law." Again, why is "Jesus in the Law" a bad thing? Didn't Paul say that the goal of the law was Jesus (Romans 10:4)? Aren't God and Jesus one? Didn't Jesus say that He revealed the Father, His will was His Father's will, and He only did what the Father told Him to do? Didn't Jesus say, "If you had known me, you would have known my Father also?" (John 14:7) So Jesus gave the Law! The instructions of Jesus are the same as the words of the Father (John 14:10, 11).

The fourth thing Bill is teaching is a form of what the Church used to call heresy, first taught by a guy named Marcion around 130 A.D. Marcion wanted to limit the Bible to the Gospels and writings of Paul and reject the rest. So does Bill. He says, "making Jesus' and Paul's instructions their life's focus" as if that's all there is to God's instructions. Nicolaitan statements like those from Mr. Perkins make me think he should rename the conference "Stealing the Mind." I'd be a great speaker for that conference. I could show exactly how Nicolaitans are stealing the mind!

The Bible tells us that the body of Jesus is one and there is only one faith (Ephesians 4:4-6). Both Gentile and Jewish people must be born again of the Spirit by grace through faith to be a part of the one body, as Jesus told Nicodemus in John 3. Gentile believers are grafted in to the Body as Paul says in Romans 9 through 11. We are "brought near" to the covenants and promises of Israel as he says in Ephesians 2:13. No one has to "work Jesus into the Law." He's already there.

Bait and Switch. Continuing to speak of Nicolaitan marketing, "bait and switch" advertising is standard. For instance, they'll offer "bible study" as if they really study the Bible. But all they really study is Church dogma according to the elemental spirits of the world. So they should call the studies "Dogma Studies." They tell us Jesus is in the Church, but much of His Word is absent, so how could Jesus be there? They say they "speak the Word" or even speak for Jesus, but they ignore His commands. Bait and switch tactics are so common in the Church that God should seriously consider suing for false advertising.

You attend their clubhouse/Church, and they're nice people and all and you like the music. They have a nursery and a vibrant youth group. Lots of people stop right there when looking for a group to join but maybe, like me, you want more of God. Our hunger and thirst is not satisfied or quenched by up tempo songs and a multi-media presentation. We need solid food (1 Corinthians 3:2; Hebrews 5:2). So you decide to attend a Sunday school class or home fellowship. You stay quiet, trying to figure out what they believe and where you stand with them. Soon the leader asks you to participate, so you give an observation or opinion. Or maybe you ask a question or two about inconsistencies in teaching, and suddenly the atmosphere changes. There seems to be a chill in the air. The more you participate, the cooler the temperature.

What they wanted was to add you to their tithe-paying flock of NPC robots.[2] Just shut up and join the choir. But by asking Bible questions they cannot answer, you shake their little house of cards. There is no searching of the Scriptures to find out whether these things are true (Acts 17:11) or testing people to discover false teachers (Revelation 2:2). There is no admitting they might be wrong. They simply reject you by labeling you "divisive" and showing you the door. Just like the Pharisees did Jesus.

I have been told both directly and indirectly a number of times to vacate the premises, or to forget Church in the first place. I discovered to my chagrin that Churches are falsely advertising they are part of the *ekklesia*. But they do not practice the truth or "make disciples of all nations...teaching them to observe all I have commanded you" (Matthew 28:19-20). What they are doing instead is building a social club with mind-numbed proselytes who are twice as much children of hell as themselves (Matthew 23:15).

The Dogma Wall. Jesus broke down the "dividing wall of hostility" between Jews and the rest of the world by abolishing the oral law or "the law of commandments expressed in ordinances" (Ephesians 2:11-22). This wall kept Jews and Gentiles from becoming one body. Nicolaitans couldn't wait to put the wall back up. The word "ordinances" is the Greek word "dogma" (Strong's 1378). I've mentioned "dogma" a few times, and according to a dictionary, dogma is "a point of view or tenet put forth as authoritative without adequate grounds." The Theological Dictionary of the New Testament (Little Kittle) defines it as "what seems to be right" along with "to affirm an opinion," and "to establish a decree" or "publish an edict." They also (wrongly) list

---

[2] NPC is an abbreviation for "non-player character." These are bystanders in video games having limited and wooden responses to give clues or directions.

"the law," because while God's Law might be considered a decree (or even an opinion), it is not the same as a decree or opinion from men. Dogma is all the junk plastered over God's Law by oral laws.

Jesus paid the price for our sin and gave believers new hearts of flesh written with the Word by the Spirit; Nicolaitans, claiming gatekeeper status, lock those hearts away from the Word behind a new stone wall of dogma. Jesus cleared the way to God; Nicolaitans throw every stumbling block they can find in the path. Jesus holds out the bread of abundant life in the living oracles of God, along with rivers of living water flowing with goodness and blessing, for those who hunger and thirst after God. Nicolaitans dam up the river and dole out meager portions of stale bread and lukewarm water, keeping believers in a constant state of near-starvation and malnutrition.

From the dietary command broken in the Garden (eating the wrong fruit), to the refusal of Israel to go into the land and later disobedience, to the persecution of prophets, to the crucifixion, to the "resistance" in Acts, to the creation by man of the Church, the issue has always been, "Will you follow God or not?" The Word from a loving, just, thrice holy, merciful, longsuffering Father is the dividing line between those in the kingdom and those outside.

Jesus is standing at the door of the Church knocking gently; Nicolaitans are on the other side holding the deadbolt closed, blocking their ears to the invitation. Happily, Jesus also has set before His friends an open door that no man, not even a Nicolaitan, can shut.

3 Logging Out

Proverbs 13:13, ESV. Whoever despises the word brings destruction on himself, but he who reveres the commandment will be rewarded.

The Fantasy. Most everyone has heard the story of the birth of the Church. How Jesus came to tell the Jews that they were all wrong and He was starting something new. He showed that The Law which they depended on for salvation was fulfilled and mostly eliminated (except for the tithe of course). But they wouldn't listen and crucified Him for daring to throw out the Old Testament. As they rejected Jesus, so Jesus rejected them. In Acts chapter 2, He gave the Holy Spirit so His apostles could go to the Gentiles and start the Church. In Acts 10 Peter was reminded that now we could eat a ham sandwich. A Church council met in Acts 15 and determined that all of the Laws except maybe the moral ones were kaput. The Church continued to preach Jesus and grew with the help of a converted Jew named Paul. The newly Christianized Paul wrote a bunch of letters to Churches correcting their tendency to follow the Law and showed them the way of salvation by grace through faith instead. Church fathers continued to help the Church grow and through many trials in the Church age, it has triumphed.

The Truth. Well, I'm going to tell you a different story I learned after I got the log out of my own eye or "logged out" of the standard Church. It is the story of the olive tree or the body of Christ. I'll use the same Bible, along with some history, but you might be surprised at how radically different the Bible story is, compared to the standard Church story. I guarantee you will be surprised at where the Church really began, who was responsible, and the truth about the body of Christ.

His story starts way back in Genesis, in the Garden. God gives a few instructions to man, along with the Sabbath, which suggests a permanent condition of rest which will come later. The pre-incarnate Jesus walked in the Garden with Adam, and one of the trees He planted was the olive tree or Body of Christ. He is the root of the olive tree. A battle began with the deceiver making partial casualties of Adam and Eve. After the fall, God promises Adam and Eve that estrangement from Him would not continue. The "seed of the woman," which we know is Jesus the Messiah, would appear and destroy the works of the deceiver (Genesis 3:15). The implication was that the deceiver would ultimately lose the battle and God would establish His kingdom instead. It would continue forever. This promise was handed down through the olive tree generations before the flood from Adam to Seth and on down to Noah. God's olive tree flourished and many were part.

The deceiver attempted to end the line of the seed of the woman by inciting Cain to fight with Able. He also managed to influence almost all of the pre-flood people away from God. They got further and further from God until He decided to cleanse the earth with water. The dove with the olive branch after the flood shows us many things, but among them is that God's Promise continues and His olive tree of believers is still in existence.

After the flood, the battle continued with the deceiver using Ham and his son Canaan, and God choosing Shem. The promise of the Messiah passed to succeeding generations, but only a few grabbed hold of God such as Abraham, Isaac, Jacob and Joseph. Jesus received tithes in the form of Melchizedek from a victorious Abraham, and later talked with Abraham about righteous people in Sodom and Gomorrah. When not enough righteous were to be found in those cities, Jesus wiped that cesspool off the planet.

The deceiver would try to build his kingdom and end the line of the Messiah, using frontal attacks with the weakness of men and the likes of Nimrod and his Tower of Babel or other kings. He created Babylon; a combination of two anti-God kingdoms, featuring control of people through indulgence of the flesh with the power of wealth and a prostitute religion. This kingdom has continued under various names and in various forms of opposition to God to the present day. Jesus saved Israel out of Egypt (Jude 5) and planted His mixed multitude olive tree in the Promised Land (Exodus). Some were natural branches, and some like Caleb (Exodus 12:38) and Rahab (Joshua 6:25) were grafted in. In addition to the Promise of His birth as a man (Deuteronomy 18:15) Jesus gave Israel a constitution or covenant (Leviticus) to live by and had them build a residence for Him. The Tabernacle was another way of looking at the promise of His eventual incarnation, as was the Ark of the Covenant. Animal sacrifices were memorials that pointed to the sacrifice the Messiah would eventually offer. Balaam was a main character in the attempt to curse the nation that cannot be cursed by man.

After the Olive Tree was planted in the Land, there was a lot of back and forth rejection of God, but also renewed commitment to Him over the next centuries. Unfruitful natural branches of the olive tree were broken off and wild olive branches (non-Jewish) were grafted in (Ruth, Matthew 1:5). During the time of the Judges, the battle went up and down but God's Promise would not be lost. The deceiver tried internal attacks such as fostering idolatry and corruption, along with external attacks from surrounding nations. God responded, when people called on His name, with the judges such as Deborah, Gideon and Samson.

The battle raged back and forth during the times of the kings of Israel, shown in the continuing cycles of rejection and renewal. Ahab (with his wife Jezebel) was one of the most wicked kings used by the deceiver in the rejection of God. God allowed the deceiver to use Assyria, Babylon, Persia, Greece and Rome in Israel's chastisement when they rejected God. Israel ended up dispersed to the four winds because of their refusal to repent completely. God cut down most of the physical olive tree but a stump remained (Isaiah 6:8-13). He repeatedly sent prophets to call the people of Israel back to the promise and the covenant and to warn the nations of impending judgment. The prophets were mostly ignored or killed, except for bright spots such as the repentance of Nineveh.

Through all this there was always a remnant of the olive tree that followed God (1 Kings 19:18; Romans 11:4), and the line of the seed of the woman continued just as God planned. David received the promise with the additional information that his son would sit on the throne forever (2 Samuel 7). God chastised Israel by leaving the Temple (Ezekiel 8-11) and eventually exiling even Judah from the Land of Israel using the Assyrians (Ephraim) and the Babylonians (Judah). Jesus still makes appearances such as in the furnace with Daniel's friends and Daniel's visions. Some Israelites managed to eventually come back to the Land. With God's help, they fought to build some semblance of a kingdom in times of trouble (as shown to Daniel) and succeeded just in time (Ezra, Nehemiah) for the Messiah. Jeremiah (31:31-34) and Ezekiel (16:59-63) emphasized the new covenant He would confirm, which would entail the writing of the Law on new hearts of flesh by the Spirit (Ezekiel 11:19-20, 36:26-27).

Somewhere in the few hundred years before Jesus was born the deceiver tried the different battle tactic of "If you can't beat 'em, join 'em." That wasn't a new tactic; he had used it successfully with idolatry and agents such as Balaam and Jezebel. But this time he worked from inside by having his people masquerade as godly leaders, adding to and subtracting from the Word. He started infiltrating his Nicolaitan or Pharisee and Sadducee agents into Israel and tempted them to create Judaism. His tactic was, if a little bit of law is good, a lot is better. So there were all sorts of rulings and interpretations made that looked good but obscured God's love and Spirit in the Law, which the deceiver hates.

God protected and sustained the genealogy of the Promised seed that the deceiver tried so hard to destroy. In His timing, the family line He preserved produced the seed of the woman who we call Jesus. The promised Messiah arrived and confirmed the promise made so long before starting with Adam and Eve.

Malachi 3:1, ESV. "Behold, I send my messenger, and he will prepare the way before me. And the Lord whom you seek will suddenly come to his temple; and the messenger of the covenant in whom you delight, behold, he is coming, says the LORD of hosts.

Jesus confirmed the covenant He made with Israel at Mt. Sinai (in the second Sermon on the Mount Matthew 5-7), by removing the heavy load of rulings, traditions and philosophies of men that covered it. He established the new covenant by filling the Law up full of love and the Spirit and handing it to Israel. But instead of rejoicing and repenting, most of the people rejected Him. Again.

The deceiver must've been dancing in the demonic streets at the crucifixion; he was probably surprised with the biggest comedown ever when Jesus resurrected. Happily, a large number of Jewish people saw the truth of the promised living Word (Jesus), embracing Him and His sacrifice. They accepted the renewal of His kingdom from inside out. The resurrection meant victory over the deceiver, and the way to God was uncluttered again for anyone who wanted to receive the Promise. Believers were grafted into a distinguished family olive tree going all the way back through Abraham to Adam. But the battle continued.

In Acts chapter 2 we see the refreshing and renewal of God's plans on earth as 3,000 law-abiding Jews were eagerly saved from that crooked generation and entered into God's kingdom. Jewish believers were added day by day, and a few weeks later 5,000 more were added. In Acts 10 Peter's erroneous view of Gentiles as dogs, taught by the Pharisees who also said only Jews had salvation, was corrected. Peter saw the light in that "in every nation anyone who fears him and does what is right is acceptable to him" (Acts 10:34-35). Non-Jewish people such as Cornelius were grafted into the olive tree in great numbers. In Acts 15, the Jewish believer council recognized that Gentiles were saved by grace through faith just as they, and all people, had always been. They recommended a few rules to help Jews and Gentiles fellowship together until the Gentiles learned Torah, taught in the synagogues every Sabbath (Acts 15:21).

A Pharisee named Paul saw the light in a manner similar to Peter when Jesus introduced Himself. Paul stopped his persecution of those he thought were against God when he discovered that Jesus-as-Messiah believers were, in fact, part of the olive tree (Romans 9-11). He went through a long education program and came out teaching that the rulings of the Jewish leaders were covering over the promise and preventing people from reaching God. This Hebrew of Hebrews, this Pharisee, a man blameless as to the righteousness under the Law (Philippians 3:1-11), taught that the Law was holy, righteous, good and spiritual (Romans 7:12, 14). He delighted in the Law (Romans 7:22) and taught that salvation had always been by grace through faith. All of which was consistent with God's message from the beginning (Galatians 3:17-21). Every letter he wrote was filled with exhortations for "keeping the commandments of God" (1 Corinthians 7:19).

The deceiver's tactic of placing false shepherds in groups of people trying to follow God worked so well with the Pharisees and Judaism, he decided to try it again with Nicolaitans and The Way. Gradually Nicolaitans inserted themselves here and there, lording it over the less educated and helping to create a Church opposed to the whole Word of God. Their marching orders were to mix as much of the deceiver's lies with as little Bible truth as possible. The idea was to steer the ship away from God while continuing to make it look like it was still sailing in the right direction. This way the deceiver could create a false body of Christ and fool people into thinking it was the real thing. His master plan was to create a Tower, like Nimrod's Tower of Babel, that would appear to be opposed to his own kingdom, yet in actuality belonged to him.

As the years rolled on, more and more Gentiles were grafted in to the olive tree of the body of Christ, and natural branches were broken off (Romans 9-11). Unbelieving Jews rebelled against Roman rule until the Romans destroyed the

Temple in 70 A. D. and Jerusalem in 135 A. D. All the books we now call the New Testament, except for the Revelation, were written before the Temple destruction.

The Roman emperor instituted a tax after the Temple was destroyed making all Jews give money to the temple of Jupiter in Rome instead. Believers up to this time were still following the Law and the Prophets, and didn't look any different from the Jews on the outside. The Romans couldn't tell believers apart from Jews so they were all included in the taxation. Believers did not want to pay the tax or die in the rebellions so they tried to find ways to differentiate themselves from the Jews. Teachings circulated among the now mostly Gentile congregations that God rejected Israel. The destruction of the Temple was used as proof that the followers of the Nazarene (Jesus) had replaced Jews.

Starting about 70 A. D. the battle got hotter for control of Jesus-believing congregations. Nicolaitan (and other false) teachings that only borrowed from the Bible were refined. Pharisees had turned God's Words into a heavy burden no Jew could bear. Gentile Pharisees that Jesus officially named Nicolaitans showed up in the Word doing the same thing in 95 A. D. when John wrote Revelation. They were some of the wolves in sheep's clothing about which Jesus (Matthew 7:15, 10:16) and the apostles (Acts 20:29) warned. They were able to infiltrate the congregations of Ephesus and Pergamum teaching things that Jesus hates. The deceiver, represented by such as the Nicolaitan, Balaam and Jezebel teachers, fought real believers such as those in Ephesus who tested false apostles. By the time Jesus dictated the seven letters, the replacement teachings along with a "new covenant" bearing no relation to the previous covenant were beginning to take hold.

The Nicolaitan teachings about "Christ killers" got a big boost when the Romans destroyed Jerusalem in 135 A. D. I think the Nicolaitan teachers were using their education to make plausible arguments against the plain meaning of the Bible text, and twisting it into something only they could understand. They "lorded over" the lay people, working to create what was going to become the Church.

Nicolaitans introduced other hated teachings in the congregations. Some such as those of Marcion were rejected, but many of the teachings hung around in dark corners. Marcion thought that there were two gods (an old bloody one and new nice one) and that the believer's Bible should only include Paul's writings and maybe one or two other select books. Most of the Christian leaders disavowed his teachings, but the two gods and abbreviated Bible and some other teachings survive in the Church to this day.

In 200 A. D., the books of the New Testament were collected together and officially recognized as being for the replacement Church. The "old covenant" was dumped on the Jews, and the unbiblical Nicolaitan "new covenant" or testament was taken for the Church. The rabbis wrote down all their rulings of the Mishnah at the same time. Both of these documents were intended to support the authority and teachings of the two types of Nicolaitans, Jewish and Gentile. The battle raged in the Church between false and true teachers until about 325 A. D. That was when the Nicolaitans under the Roman emperor Constantine won the battle for control of the new "Church." The olive tree was again mostly cut down, but remnants were scattered around the Church. The deceiver, operating from his throne in Pergamum, made it look like he lost when in fact he got the brass ring. The Church was born when officially co-opted by the Roman Empire. He couldn't beat believers, so he joined them.

God's story is continuous. There are no interruptions, no false starts, and never has God had to retrace His steps or find a new plan because the deceiver flummoxed the other plan.

Malachi 3:6, ESV. "For I the LORD do not change; therefore you, O children of Jacob, are not consumed.

Jesus has always been thousands of years ahead of anything the deceiver or man could ever throw at Him. He has always loved and always wanted man to love Him back. His elect Remnant, Olive Tree, Bride, and body of Christ has always been around, never in danger of extinction. He wins the battles, and He will win the war. This is the biblical story of the Olive Tree and the birth of the Church.

The Church's story of its birth should start with, "Once upon a time in a land far away." It is a fairy tale. The facts from the Bible are twisted and reinterpreted to justify the existence of an artificial, man-made Tower of Babel. There is no Church in the Bible, only in translations. The Nicolaitans battled believers and gradually created the Church. Now they rule it. It is supposed to be THE place for believers to go, but the deceiver is getting the last laugh about that. The Church is the deceiver's creation, led by the bad shepherds who have bought into his franchise marketing efforts. It looks like it is God's, wrapped in sheep's clothing, but it is really the opposite. The Church as we see it today is a hollow mockery of the body of Christ. It doesn't even remotely resemble the body life represented in Joshua or Acts 2. Disobedience is institutionalized; hypocrisy formalized.

You might think I'm talking about the Catholic Church only, but I'm not. It is true that the Catholic Church took the lead for many centuries. It is also true that the Protestants fought against many of the false teachings and injustices of the Catholics. But all of them have kept the fiction of The Church and its attendant Nicolaitan, Balaam and Jezebel teachings. All of them regard themselves as separate from Israel and somehow more special. Many, many Christian leaders such as Martin Luther have been, and are, anti-Jewish. Catholic and Protestant Churches, as well as many pagan religions such as Islam, are part of "Babylon the great" (Revelation 17:5). All are included in that mystery religion Babylon created by the deceiver that has battled God and His Word throughout the millennia. Judaism is included too. Many bad shepherds are trying to get people to come into the Church, but Jesus is telling His people to come out of her (Revelation 18:4). God didn't create it, it didn't replace Israel, they don't follow His ways, and the Church (or Judaism) isn't the body of Christ.

The Anointed Elite. Throughout history, there have been people who wanted to be in charge of everyone else. The people who spend their lives in pursuit of ruling other people we call elites. The elites think that they are the ones who should rule over the peasants. They say it's because they're smarter, wiser, and more knowledgeable. But really, it's because they want power and control. A respected statesman in the 1800's named Daniel Webster (I think) said of elite politicians, "They promise to rule wisely. But they mean to rule."

Most get elite status by virtue of education, experience, birth, money or popular acclaim. They don't usually get it on the strength or truth of God's Word. The deceiver finds elite people and develops them into Nicolaitans. Church Nicolaitans claim God anoints them, so we won't look too hard at their works or test them to see if they're false. But their anointing comes from their moms or almost anything other than the Word. Ordination is another way of saying anointing, except all it really means is that as long as you teach what the denomination approves, you'll keep your job and get a paycheck. If something is wrong in the Church, it must be the fault of the peasants. It's because the Church is "full of sinners"[3] or "they're not listening to us" or "we have to do Church differently" or some other cause. Never is it the result of the false teaching of the elite, anointed, ordained Nicolaitans.

All believers or churchgoers might be or have been Nicolaitans. Most of us have acted like an elite and taught against parts of the Word such as the Law at least on occasion. Maybe sometimes we've acted like Pharisees. Some of us are genuinely

---

[3] Opinion editorial on foxnews.com 11/17/18 "Church is For Sinners https://www.foxnews.com/opinion/is-church-is-for-sinners.

misled or just wrong and when we see the truth, we repent. Then there are those who are too much in love with themselves, their position, authority or a paycheck to even consider repenting. Reversing the damage unrepentant Nicolaitans cause is worth the effort of illuminating their hateful works in this book. Nicolaitans are destroying the maturity, abundant life and fruit of the Spirit in believers. If we want to get close to God, we need to test them, identify them, get away from their teachings and turn to the Word.

Wool Suits. Nicolaitans have gotten very, very good at hiding right out in the open. A lot of them teach some good things to disguise the bad. It's even possible that they get a large part of the teachings about Jesus correct. After all, even demons know the truth. They just don't embrace it. "You believe that God is one; you do well. Even the demons believe-and shudder!" (James 2:19.)

> Matthew 7:21–23, ESV. "Not everyone who says to me, 'Lord, Lord,' will enter the kingdom of heaven, but the one who does the will of my Father who is in heaven. On that day many will say to me, 'Lord, Lord, did we not prophesy in your name, and cast out demons in your name, and do many mighty works in your name?' And then will I declare to them, 'I never knew you; depart from me, you workers of lawlessness.'

Nicolaitans can be hard to spot because they use as much "sheep's clothing" as they need to disguise their error, without actually teaching the Bible. They are literally "workers of no law," also called lawlessness or iniquity, in wool suites. When you see through the wool, you might be offended that you were fooled. I was, and what made it harder was that for years I was a Nicolaitan.

I learned all the Church doctrine as well as I could, and then I taught it. I had some good teachers and mentors, people I respected and tried my best to emulate. There were lots of leaders who were (and are) caring, and taught (or teach) many good things. I thought of myself that way. But most of them just did not (and do not) teach the Bible well at all. They are teaching things like dispensationalism, amillenialism, covenantalism, creeds, social justice (by their own definition), white privilege, anti-racism, aborting (which we could also call sacrificing) babies, global warming, "you can be as God," socialism and all sorts of other rubbish. If they just taught the whole Word of God, the Church might actually look like the congregation of Acts 2.

I know their tactics and philosophies backwards and forwards because that was I, except for the liberal junk. I focused on the conservative/evangelical junk. I believed and taught doctrine such as dispensationalism, the Church as a separate entity from Israel, the Old Testament Law was mostly fulfilled and eliminated by Jesus and related subjects. I found out later these teachings were not in the Bible. Just philosophies of men sprinkled with a few verses to make them look holy.

Psalm 119:99, ESV. I have more understanding than all my teachers, for your testimonies are my meditation.

You might realize you are a Nicolaitan too. Don't be upset though, because there is always time to "log out." It was a hard process for me to repent and learn what the Bible really says. If you find yourself in the same condition, it's not too late.

Jesus told me to take the log out of my own eye so I can see clearly to take the speck out of my brother's eye (Matthew 7:3-5). After I "logged out" of standard Church doctrine, however, I see a big piece of timber hanging by a thread about ready to drop on the head of my brothers. I'm saying, "Um, you might want to move out from under that tree about to fall on you." But they refuse. Or they resent my audacity in even mentioning it. Just because we see clearly that does not mean the effort to help our brothers improve their vision will be successful. We can look forward to about the same success as Jesus had with most Pharisees.

Plague of Biblical Proportions. Nicolaitan politicians clamor for the power to tell people what to do without the restraint of something like the U. S. Constitution because they "know better." Nicolaitan doctors are demanding that patients stop questioning their treatments (such as vaccinations) and just do what they say because they "know better." Nicolaitan priests, pastors, popes, ministers and rabbis demand that followers quit reading and doing God's Word and just follow their lead. The reason is, you guessed it, they "know better." This is why I call Nicolaitans a plague of biblical proportions. We are drowning in man's knowledge; the fruit of the wrong tree in the Garden.

Nicolaitan elites start out, perhaps, with good intentions. Study hard, try to learn as much as you can about the subjects, and then try to help people with your knowledge. A few manage to stick to good principles and really do help. Most do not. Instead, they use the trust they may earn to teach falsehoods and force behavior changes to those more in line with their own personal opinions. When we reject God's Word, He turns us over to these elites with stubborn hearts. In a way, we ask for this plague because we have itching ears.

Psalm 81:11–12, ESV. "But my people did not listen to my voice; Israel would not submit to me. So I gave them over to their stubborn hearts, to follow their own counsels.

Too many elites have abused the trust placed in them by using it to manipulate people instead of helping them. Man-caused climate change is one such example of manipulation into which some Church Nicolaitans have plunged. Oh, not that the climate doesn't change, but it is demonstrated by facts that man is not responsible. Still the elites repeat the mantra over and over. There was the "eat no fat" diet and cholesterol preaching in the '80's. The experts said fat caused heart disease, only to find out recently that the near-absence of fat in a diet might very well be a main cause of Alzheimer's. We can add the panic over too much salt in the diet, so-called renewable energy like solar and wind, pesticides like DDT, population growth, vaccines, vegans, and on and on. In almost every case, the experts turn out to be wrong. "Consensus" from wrong "experts" inside and outside the Church has made me leery of all those people who "know better." As God has said, "The heart is deceitful above all things, and desperately wicked: who can know it?" (Jeremiah 17:9 AV).

When it comes to the Bible, just about anyone can call himself or herself an expert. Atheists profess expertise in the Bible, whether they admit it or not. They must be experts if they can summarily decree that there is no God.

The Church is loaded with Nicolaitan elites (and perhaps surprisingly, atheists) claiming to interpret God's Words correctly, speak for Jesus, and help save people. But like most actors and scientists nowadays, they are pushing their personal agenda more than sharing whatever knowledge they may have to help people. These Church or denominational agendas may have some of the Bible in them but are not the Bible message in its balanced completeness.

Sometimes Nicolaitans are nice teachers; mostly they are rather arrogant. You don't have to be a terrible person to be a Nicolaitan; just a little error is enough. A few Nicolaitans are close to the truth and I hope they see and repent. Many nice guys and gals are too stuck in pride and will not repent. They prefer mixing the truth of the Word into plausible arguments with philosophy, empty deceit and comfortable lies of their own making.

I'm not saying all shepherds, or even all Nicolaitans, are bad. I'm saying compare their works to the Bible. Some of the good experts, sticking with Bible principles, have put in fantastic efforts in educating themselves and translating the original languages of the Bible, sometimes even giving their lives for it. We can easily gain much from their efforts by buying a printed Bible, or even better purchasing Bible study software. It is easy to forget the strain and persecution that was involved (and in many areas still is involved) in bringing us copies of the Word of God.

Remember to say prayers of thanks for the people who lay down their lives to bring us His Word. Their efforts mean we don't have to be experts to get most of the meaning of God's Word.

Godly translators have done the hard work so we can easily access God's instructions to us in plain, easy to understand language. All we have to do is read and follow it. Just make sure to compare translations, use study helps with care, and do what it says.

I am sure that my naming some names in this book will cause hard feelings somewhere. I feel you. We need to spell out what is happening though, because the Nicolaitan teachings are so tricky. I've seen so many people damaged by the dogma preached, that if some of the leaders I name are hurt in turn then it's only fair. Jesus didn't mince words when condemning the Pharisees or the works of the Nicolaitans. I think that calling people out for their domineering philosophies of men is right in line with His focus.

More Clues. I've referred to the seven letters of Revelation a little bit. In summary, we know that there were seven actual congregations addressed in those seven Asian cities, now called western Turkey. It's also probable that these are representative of seven types of congregations as well as seven types of believers throughout the ages. Looking at the Church now, I think we can still see the seven types of congregations and types of believers.

More information concerning the seven congregations and perhaps the Nicolaitans is in the books of Ephesians, Colossians, and 1 & 2 Timothy. Paul wrote these books a few decades before Revelation, but the seeds of some of the problems addressed by Jesus later in the seven letters are evident. From those seeds, we can gain some insight into Nicolaitan fruit. Let's take a closer look.

Colossians and Laodicea. The book of Colossians was to be exchanged with a letter to the congregation of Laodicea (Colossians 4:16) which we don't have. The cities were only a few miles apart, so Colossae and Laodicea might have had similar problems. Laodicea eventually (in Revelation) had severe problems with lukewarm works and what seems to be wealth, and were reproved and disciplined by Jesus in Revelation 3:14-22. Laodicea was where Jesus was standing at the door and knocking. If any were to "hear his voice and open the door" (see also John

10:3-5) He will "come in to him and eat with him," so they were pretty far gone. It's funny in a sad way that so many use these words when speaking to the unsaved about salvation. But Jesus isn't knocking for the unsaved; He's knocking for the Church.

Paul in the Colossae letter spends some time warning against "plausible arguments" and "philosophy and empty deceit, according to human tradition, according to the elemental spirits of the world, and not according to Christ." Modern Nicolaitans try to make this about the Word or the Law, but the descriptions don't match. Paul is talking about human tradition contrary to the Word, not the Word itself. In Colossians 2:18 he specifically says "let no one disqualify you," which relates back to 2:16 "with regard to a festival or new moon or Sabbath." Paul was obviously encouraging the believers to continue with their practice of the Word and to refuse to let the philosophies of men deter them.

In Colossians 2:21-22 Paul speaks of "regulations - 'Do not handle, Do not taste, Do not touch'...according to human precepts and teachings." Again, the Nicolaitans (then and now), in their zeal to promote the Church as a new and unique entity, try to link these verses to the Word of God, and the Law in particular, when they have nothing to do with it. Paul says so right there in verse 22 - "human precepts and teachings." This isn't the Word; it is the very thing the Nicolaitan teaches! The Nicolaitan is saying that there are extra-biblical rules for being holy, such as those connected with asceticism (like the Amish). What I'm saying, and what Paul says, is don't let men's regulations get in the way of your practice of the Word.

Going "according to Christ" for Paul (and me) means to do what the Christ commanded. Jesus gave the Law at Mount Sinai, and believers are supposed to make disciples and "teach them to obey all I commanded." We are supposed to live and teach the Word along with the clarifying commands He and the apostles gave. We want to stick to what is written (1 Corinthians 4:6), not to all of the extra regulations created by men.

Jesus doesn't mention the Nicolaitans directly in the Revelation note to Laodicea, or in the Colossian letter. But we have the extensive warnings in Colossians about philosophies of men and elemental spirits. It seems that false teachers were already a problem in Colossae, and that is the case probably in Laodicea too. The false teachers may have had more success in Laodicea if the note in Revelation is any indication, or both cities are so closely associated that the note to Laodicea is sufficient for both.

Ephesians and Timothy. In the book of Ephesians Paul speaks of love 14 times (rooted and grounded in love 3:17), walking worthy, the dividing wall of hostility broken down (2:14), and one body (Gentiles brought near 2:13, one body 4:4-6). A dividing wall was in the Temple court that divided Jews from Gentiles. Paul made a comparison between this literal wall (not commanded by God), with the dividing wall of dogma in the oral law, which also divides Gentiles and Jews. Both walls were hostile to Gentiles, and Jesus destroyed each of them.

Paul instructed Timothy, the leader of the Ephesian congregations, to keep love going and warned him about some who "will depart from the faith by devoting themselves to deceitful spirits and teachings of demons." The Ephesians only listened to Paul and Timothy for a while, because about 30 years later Jesus said they had abandoned the love they had at first. He also encouraged them to do the "works you did at first." On the up side, godly Ephesians were holding off the Nicolaitans who had departed from the faith, and hated their works. They also still tested false apostles and did not bear with those who were evil.

So to recap a little, Paul warns the Ephesians that wolves will arise from inside their leadership speaking twisted things. Later, he instructs the Ephesians 14 times about love, the removal of hostility in the broken dividing wall, and one body. He encourages Timothy to watch for those who depart from sound teaching and to keep the commandment. The Colossians, neighbors of Laodicea and Ephesus, need to avoid philosophies of men because they disqualify believers from following God's Laws. Jesus later says the Ephesians lost love, and identifies two of the wolves in Ephesus as Balaam and the Nicolaitans. The word "Nicolaitan" means ruling over lay people. I think the case is clear that loveless Nicolaitans were ruling over believers with philosophies of men, which included the replacement doctrines separating Jews and Gentiles, rather than the Bible.

We can't say for sure if the "twisted things" Paul warns about came from Nicolaitans, or produced the Nicolaitans. But we *can* say if it quacks like a duck, walks on webbed feet like a duck, has feathers and a bill and lays eggs like a duck, it's a duck. In other words, if someone elevates twisted things (the philosophies of men) over the Bible, there is no doubt they belong to the group of false teachers.

Our modern Nicolaitans are "from among your own selves" and "fierce wolves" too. To this day, the Church promotes separation from Jews, instead of one body, with their own oral laws. So if a person gives us plausible arguments insisting that we should believe him or her without support from the Bible; if they allow elemental spirits of the world with sexual immorality or Jesus idolatry; if they shut down biblical questions; if they lock away the Old Testament behind a dogma wall of "fulfilled and eliminated;" if they defend themselves as being the "anointed" of God; or if they talk a lot about Jesus but don't do what He says, then we have a duck. Err, I mean a Nicolaitan.

The Apostles. The key difference between a leader such as an apostle and a Nicolaitan is that the apostles (and all other true teachers) point people to the Word of God. Nicolaitans point people away. As I said, Paul, for instance, tells us "not to go beyond what is written" (1 Corinthians 4:6). Jesus called it the Law and the Prophets, and modern Nicolaitans insist we call it the Old Testament. Paul obviously wanted believers to follow the written Word of God. John says that "Whoever keeps his commandments abides in God and God in him. And by this we know he abides in us, by the Spirit whom he has given us" (1 John 3:24).

A Nicolaitan does the opposite. I'll talk more about this in chapter 5, but here I will say they point you away from much of the Word, except perhaps as inspirational stories or psalms. "Love" for them is limited to mere sentiment or feelings alone. This way they can seem to be encouraging people to follow Jesus, when in reality they steer them towards an attitude of "if it feels good, do it." They remove the objective standard of the Law and the Prophets and replace it with feelings they can manipulate.

One of the other big differences between apostles and Nicolaitans is that the apostles were by and large eye-witnesses of the acts of Jesus, and merely testified to what they had seen. They directed people to the Word of God for faith and living. They did not "lord it over" people, but humbly revealed what they knew to be true. Believers heeded the apostle's teachings only as they passed the test of the Word (Revelation 2:2).

Their works, on the other hand, link Nicolaitans and Pharisees together. They do not adhere to the Word, and use the authority of their self-anointed position to force the acceptance of traditions and teachings not in keeping with the Bible. Nicolaitans may not be obvious about force in modern times because they don't use whips as they used on Jesus and the apostles. Or they don't use the Inquisition which the Catholic Church inflicted on those they considered heretics. Instead, they use the force of their education, money, Facebook likes, bestselling books, the Church fathers, history, denominational backing, excommunication or the large population of their mega-Churches to change, suppress and otherwise block access to the truth of the Word of God.

As we'll see in the following pages, Nicolaitans make assertions with no backup from the Word, using words from the Bible but putting them together in a way that abolishes the meaning. Nicolaitans teach many of the basic doctrines of Jesus and God, but not the way the Bible teaches. There are parts of good things from the Bible in much of their teaching. However, they lock away the believer from maturity in Christ when they forbid the practice of large portions of the Word, such as the Law.

James says that not many should be teachers (James 3:1) because they will be judged with greater strictness. They are also subject to the millstone effect (Matthew 18:6), and there really is only one Teacher. If people teach, they need to be careful to humbly teach and live the words of God. It is best to avoid pet doctrines or traditions that interfere with His living oracles.

Isaiah 30:20, ESV. And though the Lord give you the bread of adversity and the water of affliction, yet your Teacher will not hide himself anymore, but your eyes shall see your Teacher.

4 Grasping for Power

Psalm 119:128, ESV. Therefore I consider all your precepts to be right; I hate every false way.

Though there isn't any direct information in the Bible about Nicolaitan teachings, I've drawn conclusions from biblical evidence. Now I'm going to make some connections from the fruit of men grasping for power. Nicolaitans need power for domineering. In this chapter, I'll look at examples of their power or authority grabs from history, rabbinic Judaism, the treatment of Jesus at the Incarnation, and the book of Acts. We will also refer to the Catholic Church and current behavior of the Protestant Church. Stay with me here because the information will be helpful in understanding the ancient, and the modern, Nicolaitans.

Matthew 7:15, ESV. "Beware of false prophets, who come to you in sheep's clothing but inwardly are ravenous wolves.

Misusing Authority. In any group of people in almost any circumstance, leaders will emerge. Some Church leaders will point to God and follow Him, but many only look like they are pointing to Him. These hypocrites will plot, scheme and scrabble to get the authority or ego feeding they crave, and then misuse it for their own ends. They might be convinced they are right or even biblical, they might just be misled, but pride of place is common because of education, wealth or other forms of worldly success.

Church elites usually add an "anointed" qualification, measured by the reception of their teachings. Teachings don't have to match the Bible; just make sure to toss in a few well-worn Bible phrases. Not too much truth, though, because I've heard many times from pastors that the flock just can't handle the meat of the Word, even after years of their teaching. But if a lot of people "like" your teachings, or agree with them or get all tingly when hearing them, then you must be "anointed." If you build a mega-church or have hundreds of people pay for one of your conferences, well then you also are "anointed." Believers who stand alone for the truth, like Jeremiah, must not have it then.

We can see the fruit of authority misuse playing out all through the Bible and history in general. Power is the name of the game. Part of Cain's issue with Abel was power. Nimrod wanted control over the earth. Joseph's brothers didn't want to bow down to their younger brother. Wicked kings, tyrants and dictators all want control over everyone around them. The Pharisees loved control and power; Nicolaitans rose up with similar goals. Catholic priests grab for it and many other Church leaders hunger for it.

Nicolaitan wolves have all sorts of ear-tickling styles and methods to gain Church power or feed the ego. Most of the methods and styles are very complex, because explaining away the plain truth of God's Word requires quite a bit of complicated twisting and turning. Sort of like the way a snake moves in grass.

Modern Nicolaitans attack the authority of God and the Word by mixing truth and lies. Their arguments sound and look good, appealing to the natural desires in man; what Paul calls the flesh. Or like Jezebel of Thyatira, they might add a claim of some special authority from God marked by healings, prophecies or other lying signs and wonders (Ezekiel 13:17-23). Whatever the claims, the way of men (or women) is to gain power or control over you so they can feed their pride, or their wallets, and be "like God" or "boast in your flesh" (Galatians 6:13). They misuse their authority to dodge God's Word, especially the Law, in many ways.

Once they have cast doubt on the plain meaning of God's Word, either because they say it's too complicated (or you're too dumb), they have inserted themselves between it and you. Then you have to go to them all the time to find out the meaning. What you read isn't the meaning; the meaning is what they say it is. After they've pried you away from the plain meaning of the written Word and hooked you on listening to only their teaching, they can add you to their kingdom.

The way of men is to grab authority using education or other influence and build their kingdoms while locking you out of God's. In modern times, they develop bureaucracies (remember, "rule by desk") with clerks (a word related to "clerics" or clergy) who perpetuate philosophies of men, lock people into the Church, and keep them away from God's blessings of maturity, abundant life and the fruit of the Spirit. They preach a "personal relationship with Jesus" and at the same time deny access to all of His Words, thus keeping people dependant on the Church.

Rabbinic Judaism. No one knows the origins of Rabbinic Judaism. The roots of it are lost in the few hundred years before the Incarnation of Jesus. Priests, prophets, elders and scribes were around for a long time, but after the Diaspora, or dispersion, started officially in 597 B. C. by Babylon, they became more important. Many Levites led Israel into idolatry (1 Samuel 2:12), but some, such as the sons of Zadok Ezekiel mentions (44:15) stayed true to God. Israel's leaders generally misused the power and authority entrusted to them, and the Pharisees or rabbis were no exception.

When they built the second temple and restored Jerusalem about 500 years before the Incarnation, the returning Jewish exiles needed some teaching. Levites provided it. You can read about one of the instances where Levites read from the Torah and helped people understand the Law in Nehemiah 8:7-8. The leaders of Israel are described as shepherds in places such as Ezekiel 34. Gradually, over a few hundred years, rabbis emerged, perhaps from village elders who studied Torah if a Levite wasn't available. Synagogues naturally formed where people gathered to learn.

People went to these shepherds not only for learning the Torah but also for learning how to live it. Pride wasn't far behind; hard hearts developed. As I said before, rabbis interpret the Law, make rulings about the Law, and seek earnestly for ways to shore up their claimed authority by implementing more man-made laws. Their oral law is on the same level as, and frequently overrides, the written Word of God. It's very important to note that Judaism, like the Church, is a religion that uses the Bible but is not itself biblical, because of all the extra rulings. Jesus threatened the power of the rabbi's man-made religion (John 11:47-48), so they had to eliminate Him. There are Jewish believers in God that follow Him with all their heart, and then there are believers in Judaism itself which is much different. There are also churchgoers who believe in God, and others who believe in the Church instead.

Oral law, or Mishnah, wasn't in written form until 200 A. D. Perhaps coincidentally, that's also when the books of the New Testament were collected and first called the New Testament. Both writings helped strengthen and separately identify each group, Judaism and Church. Both are guilty of rebuilding a "dividing wall" (Ephesians 2:14) when there is only one Body of Christ.

Commentary called Talmud was added on to the Mishnah till about 600 A. D. Rabbinic Judaism was formalized also around 600 A.D., but the elites were ruling Judaism with the contents of the Talmud long before. Israel has had its problems with Nicolaitans since Jacob's 12 sons. Most Jewish Nicolaitans refused to recognize Jesus at Mt. Sinai, at the Incarnation, or even now.

The Treatment of Jesus. We get more clues about the Nicolaitans and power from the treatment of Jesus by different leaders in Judaism, during the time of the Incarnation. We can see some of this grasping for power in the conflicts between Jesus, the Pharisees, the Sadducees, and the scribes. It is more proper to speak of "Judaisms" at the time of Jesus walking among us than a single Judaism, because there were (and are) a number of different sects of Judaism believing different things. Just like today in the Church. Other groups at that time were priests and Levites, the Zealots who wanted a military solution to Roman rule and were disappointed that Jesus didn't agree, the Greek Jews or Hellenists, and the Essenes who wrote or preserved the Dead Sea scrolls and who expressed disgust with the religious system by living apart.

The Pharisees were Nicolaitans, just with a different name. They were the educated; the people who "knew better." Paul said this about his colleagues.

Romans 2:17–20, ESV. But if you call yourself a Jew and rely on the law and boast in God and know his will and approve what is excellent, because you are instructed from the law; and if you are sure that you yourself are a guide to the blind, a light to those who are in darkness, an instructor of the foolish, a teacher of children, having in the law the embodiment of knowledge and truth,...

This is how the Pharisees thought of themselves, and they treated Jesus badly because they were arrogant and lorded their knowledge over others (John 12:41-43). The treatment of Jesus by the Pharisees or Sadducees is similar to that which today's believers suffer at the hands of Church leaders. There are exceptions, but as a group, leaders call themselves believers and say they know His will and are guides for the blind and so on. They too are arrogant. They too lord their knowledge over others.

The study of Torah took a while, because by the time of Jesus the rabbi's interpretations of the Law had hardened into many weighty traditions that placed a heavy, burdensome yoke on the Jews. The mentions of the Law in the New Testament are generally the Torah or Old Testament combined with the oral law. In the mind of the rabbi, they were not separate. This combination was the "yoke...that neither our fathers nor we have been able to bear" in Acts 15:10, and the "yoke of slavery" spoken of by Paul in Galatians 5:1. The Word wasn't the problem. It was men.

As I said before, when Jesus tangled with the religious leaders of the first century, it wasn't because they taught the Bible and He was changing it to something new. He had been tangling with them for centuries over every word He spoke. No, the disagreements between Jesus and the leaders were over the oral law, five times negatively called "traditions" by Jesus (Matthew 15:3, 6; Mark 7:8, 9, 13), three times called "traditions of the elders" (Matthew 15:2, Mark 7:3,5) and once referred to by Mark as "many other traditions" (Mark 7:4). Jesus said several times that the leaders "set aside" "broke" (Matthew 15:3 ESV) "make void" (Matthew 15:6 ESV) "leave" (Mark 7:8 ESV) "transgressed" (Matthew 15:3 AV) or "rejected" the commandment of God in order to establish their traditions (Mark 7:9, 13).

All of the contention between Jesus and Pharisees, Sadducees, and scribes was over oral law rather than the Word. In fact, in context with the rest of the Word, we can say that God had been contending with Israel's leaders going the wrong way for a long time. Fix it firmly in mind that the spats with Jesus were just the most recent. Jesus would teach the Word, the leaders responded with their rulings. The leaders attacked Jesus with their rulings; He responded with the Word. Rabbinical interpretations of the word included such things as not healing on the Sabbath, harvesting hands full of grain on the Sabbath, eating with unwashed hands and more. But they missed the point of God's Word on many occasions. None of the traditions noted were correct interpretations of the Word. Jesus was only too happy to help them understand. Sadly, the Pharisees were not happy to receive correction, so they handed Him over to the Romans for crucifixion.

The yoke of traditions, or oral law, robs the Word of God of the love of God, and His Spirit, and does nothing to address our sin nature. And as with all teachings that include error, they increase our labor and make our burdens heavier. "Freedom in Christ" (Galatians 2:4-5, 5:1, 13) means that believers are free from the rabbi-made laws, not God's Word. The rabbi's rulings have "an appearance of wisdom in promoting self-made religion and asceticism and severity to the body, but they are of no value in stopping the indulgence of the flesh" as Paul says of unbiblical tradition in Colossians 2:23. The yoke of Jesus, also known as the Word of God (or Law and the Prophets) and the "living oracles" (Acts 7:38), filled up full with love and the Spirit, is easy and His burden is light. It's no wonder the religious leaders of that time (or any time really) had so many problems with Jesus. He threatened their position, authority, power and pride (John 11:45-57).

That doesn't mean that all rabbis are bad, or that all leaders are bad. There are some good ones here and there. The Mishnah, with the Talmud (commentary on the Mishnah), has a great deal of good teaching in it. Many rabbis such as Nicodemus and Paul embraced the living oracles from God. Both of these, and others, could at one time be termed Nicolaitans. The difference is they were willing to listen to God and repent. Most other Nicolaitans are too full of pride to either truly listen to the Word or change their ways to conform to it.

The Book of Acts. We can see the ongoing conflict all through the book of Acts between powerful elders, holding to their traditions, and the believers in Jesus as the Messiah. Both Jewish (like Alexander Acts 19:33) and non-Jewish (like Demetrius the silversmith in Acts 19:24) Nicolaitans worked together. They persecuted believers, arrested them, beat them, sometimes killed them (or plotted to kill them) and worked very hard to try and shut them up. They didn't stop with killing Jesus; they had to eliminate all opposition to their mystery religions.

Stephen gives us an epic indictment of a Nicolaitan, except he directed it at the time to Jewish religious leaders.

> Acts 7:51–53, ESV. "You stiff-necked people, uncircumcised in heart and ears, you always resist the Holy Spirit. As your fathers did, so do you. Which of the prophets did your fathers not persecute? And they killed those who announced beforehand the coming of the Righteous One, whom you have now betrayed and murdered, you who received the law as delivered by angels and did not keep it."

Pharisees and Nicolaitans are the same because both groups resist the Holy Spirit. Nicolaitans (Jew and Gentile), though they weren't called that at the time, chased Paul from town to town trying to shut him up. "Five times I received at the hands of the Jews the forty lashes less one. Three times I was beaten with rods.

Once I was stoned" (2 Corinthians 11:24-25). They killed Stephen and cast out Jesus believers from the synagogue. They stirred up rebellion against the Romans, brought false accusations against believers, and ultimately caused the destruction of the Temple and eventually Jerusalem. They were instrumental in the formation of the Church. On the other hand, there were leaders who swallowed their pride, repented and embraced Jesus and His Law.

The Catholic Church. As I said in my story of the birth of the Church, God didn't create it. The Church is not the Body of Christ. The Body follows the living oracles of God as best as they know with all their heart, knowledge and ability; the Church refuses even when shown their errors. There are many parts of the Body of Christ scattered like salt throughout the Church, but the Body is not the Church.

The word "Church" is not in the Greek or Hebrew; only in English translations. The Greek word ἐκκλησία or ekklesia (a-klay-zee-uh), rendered "Church" in most translations, simply means an assembly or congregation. The word "church" is in the translations just so the Church can grab power and identity. The Church is not the same thing as the ekklesia. Gentiles trying to define themselves as something new and different and wonderful created the Church in opposition to Judaism, but neither of them are truly godly. Some translators try to reinforce the idea of "The Church" so they translate ekklesia as "Church."

We can see the beginning of the Church in the letters to the seven congregations with the emergence of Nicolaitans, along with the teachings of Jezebel and Balaam. The anti-Jesus, anti-Semitic weeds spread until they took over and got official recognition from the Roman Empire in 325 A.D. Then the Church really took off. Historians call this period "The Parting of the Ways."

As I said before, the Church formed over several hundred years, in part as a reaction to the rejection of Jesus by Jewish leaders, and in part as a reaction from Roman persecution of the Jews. The Roman persecution took the form of destruction of the

Temple, and eventually Jerusalem, after rebellions led by the Zealots. There was also the tax I mentioned called the *fiscus judaicus* instituted by the Romans after the destruction of the Temple, which forced Jews to give money to the temple of Jupiter in Rome. Things like this drove believers who looked like Jews (and sometimes were Jews), because they followed the written instructions from God, to try and distance themselves from Israel.

The Church, officially born in 325 A.D. and led at first by a powerful Gentile Nicolaitan by the name of Emperor Constantine, made all sorts of changes to Bible practice. Like a rabbi in a toga, He declared that the Sabbath was Sunday. Then the Nicolaitans mixed some pagan holidays with a few Bible stories which eventually became Christmas and Easter. They instituted a bizarre communion service where they claimed wafers and wine became the actual body and blood of Jesus. You had to continually take it for salvation. Later they elevated the pope to infallibility, and forbade marriage to priests (1 Timothy 4:3) among other strange traditions. Excommunication, usually for questioning the authority of the Church, meant a loss of salvation because churchgoers couldn't participate in Holy Communion.

Over time, Church leaders made the same mistakes as the rabbis, setting up a ruling class of priests (Nicolaitans), developing their own unbiblical traditions, and lording their position over the rest of the flock. The seeds sown by the Nicolaitans of Ephesus and Pergamum flowered into full fruit with the Roman Catholic Church. It has the same hated teachings, same tactics and the same strategies; just different labels.

The Protestant Church. We won't single out the Catholics, however. The Protestants starting with the Reformation mostly made the same authority grabs too. They got rid of the pope, Cardinals and nuns, but exchanged them for bishops, pastors, ministers, boards and other Nicolaitan bureaucrats. On the good side, most of them ditched the mysticism of the Holy Communion and the infallibility of the pope. On the bad side, they also kept many unbiblical traditions created by the Catholic Church. Then they wouldn't look too different and could still call themselves Church. And they were still largely anti-Jewish.

There are many things Protestants have in common with Catholics still, such as a Sunday Sabbath that only superficially resembles the Sabbath given to believers by Jesus. They also meet on Sundays and reject God's feasts to practice Christmas and Easter. But one of the main things they have in common is the false idea that Jesus created something new called "the Church" that supposedly replaced Israel. Nicolaitans have worked very hard to see and teach the Church in the Bible, but it just doesn't exist.

The Nicolaitans of the Catholic Church developed and refined the idea that the Church is a separate entity, and the Nicolaitan Protestants have kept that idea going. Even now, you can see a lot of opinion editorials and other articles defending the Church. Or they lament problems in the Church with an eye towards involving more Churchgoers in social issues. Lots of them keep trying to get people to come "back to Church." Not back to the Word, back to Church. That's an important difference.

When Stephen said "You who received the law as delivered by angels and did not keep it" (Acts 7:53) he could've been talking about the modern Church Nicolaitans who do the same thing. They receive the Old Testament as delivered by angels but refuse to keep it. They might dress up their refusal by preaching all sorts of good things about Jesus, but their version of Jesus does not include the follow-through to obeying the Law He gave at Mt. Sinai. They stop at what a loving thing He did on the cross, and do not go past the cross to what it means biblically to live for Him in return.

A lot of Nicolaitans have to defend and uphold the Church because their jobs depend on it. Like Balaam, money is the motivator (see also the Pharisees Luke 16:14). If any of them, in any denomination or para-Church organization, departs from the accepted "orthodox" dogma of that denomination or para-Church organization they lose their jobs. A Baptist pastor cannot start teaching that the Law of Moses is a valid lifestyle and discipleship method for believers because he would be canned almost instantly. Do you know how this would happen? A member of the Church would call the home office of the "franchise" (the denomination) and report it. A Nicolaitan would investigate, and then fire the pastor. So pastors or ministers have to please both the flock and the bureaucrats. Church members also work as home office agents to help everything stay "orthodox."

Decades ago, I thought Calvary Chapel was really trying to change things. They claimed to follow the Holy Spirit, and the sermons included a lot of Scripture reading. Sadly, I discovered that they weren't following the Holy Spirit; they were following Chuck Smith. Yes, he was another one of the Nicolaitans.

I remember listening to Chuck on his radio show a few years ago. When a man called in and started to suggest that the Law could be a valid lifestyle for believers, Chuck hung up on him. He didn't talk about it, didn't explain. He just went on with the show. It was a classic Nicolaitan response to biblical inquiry.

My granddaughter has attended several different Church youth groups, and she stays quiet about her whole Bible beliefs. But she reveals some of her beliefs when she refuses to eat pork such as sausage or pepperoni. On the upside, people have generally been sensitive and tried to help her by ordering cheese pizzas or cooking a hamburger patty instead of a sausage patty for breakfast. On the down side, she's been "helped" by several pastors trying to teach her that "we don't have to do the law anymore." One leader at a Missionary Alliance Church gave a whole lesson to the entire youth group on the same subject, probably because of her presence. I had to intervene with two pastors to politely explain where she was coming from. Happily, they were accepting of her, but not in agreement with whole Bible beliefs. That's the point. They can't agree or they'll lose their jobs.

The parents of a lady my son dated told him that he needed to return to "accepted Protestant doctrine" when they heard he didn't want to observe Christmas and Easter in his own home. This was sadly humorous considering there was adultery and divorces in that family. It seems "accepted Protestant doctrine" includes sexual immorality such as was taught by Balaam and Jezebel. What I want you to see is that they didn't say, "Return to the Bible." They said, "Return to Protestant doctrine." The Bible wasn't the point. They solidly bought into the idea that somehow, the "Church" is right and those outside the Church are wrong. The Church has become an idolatrous Tower of Babel, with the focus on an identity separate from God's Word.

If one does see truth contrary to the non-biblical Church dogma and takes the plunge to leave, one is a "cult." My mom says I'm a cult leader and I brainwashed my family. She doesn't have anything biblical; she just says it because I'm not like her (Baptist) Church. Really, Mom? I'm following the whole Word of God. You and your Church tell me not to follow. So who is the real cult leader? Your pastor, perhaps, who teaches only part of the Bible? Could it be Church leaders corrupting the plain meaning of the Word and locking it away behind a wall of "Protestant doctrine?" Isn't the real "cult" those people in the Churches who claim a special anointing, and cherry-pick the Word to support organizations that don't follow the living oracles of God? How many shepherds indulge in sexual immorality, adultery and divorce? How many leaders leave a Church and it falls apart because it is built on the personality of the pastor and not the Bible?

Yes, some really do start real cults featuring idolatry and ignoring God's Word. But people who follow the whole truth of the Word are lumped together with them in order to protect "the Church." As if the Church wasn't a cult. A cult doesn't follow all of God's Word. Where does that leave the Church?

A very large chunk of Church teachings and traditions are for the specific purpose of supporting, protecting and expanding Church power. You can see examples all over. For instance, the advertising for a book by Nicolaitan Francis Chan declares he wants us to "treat the Church as sacred again." The Church, however, is not sacred. The Body of Christ is the sacred elect, the bride, and the olive tree. Mr. Chan sees a separate identity for "the Church" just like the Jews see a separate identity for Judaism. Separate identity from the Bible, that is. Are you starting to see the connections between Judaism, the Church and Nicolaitans?

The Believer's Authority. Believers confess their sin to God, accepting the payment for it provided by the only begotten Son of God in His blood. A small return on that is to live life by all the Words of God including His Law, showing fruit of the Spirit as they go. There are failures, and a need for confession and cleansing like Jesus showed when He washed the apostle's feet (John 13). Occasionally we need renewals of commitment here and there. The general trend, however, is unwavering commitment to the truth. Authority resides in the plain meaning of the whole Word of God.

A churchgoer, on the other hand, may have started like a believer in some respects, but has settled into living life by their own mind and will modified by whatever church creed they happen to support. Bible text is cherry-picked or forced into cubbyholes safely out of the way. Allegiance to the pastor and group-think prevents them from recognizing or adjusting to the truth of the Word. Authority is in Church leaders rather than the Bible. Add some pride, and maybe a calling from mom, and you've got fertile ground for producing more and more Nicolaitans.

5 How They Teach

> Zechariah 8:16–17, ESV. These are the things that you shall do: Speak the truth to one another; render in your gates judgments that are true and make for peace; do not devise evil in your hearts against one another, and love no false oath, for all these things I hate, declares the Lord."

In this section, I'll present the part of my case illuminating many tactics the Nicolaitans use to separate people from God's Word. I'm writing in generalities here because there are so many false teachings, it would be hard to include a detailed list. I've divided their teachings under the headings of how they teach (tactics and strategy) and what they teach (philosophies of men in the next chapter).

Introduce doubt. As I said in the previous chapter, Nicolaitans use a number of tactics to confuse and cause us to doubt God's Word. One is to say that the Bible is too difficult for the average person to understand. Even if they don't say so directly, they imply it because why else would the pastor or priest need to do all the pulpit teaching? Many teachers won't even let their flocks read the Word at all. I remember my wife had a Catholic friend for a while who was surprised that she would read the Bible herself. The friend maintained that a priest had to give her the meaning, and so she couldn't read it without him. It was humorous when my wife gently argued her friend's priest to a standstill, mostly because my wife read the Word and the priest didn't! All he knew was Catholic dogma.

The main tool for making the Word more difficult to understand is spiritualizing. This means to pretty much ignore the plain meaning and find "spiritual" meanings behind the words. We can't just read it ourselves; we have to ask the elite for meaning. You can recognize this when you ask a question and the Nicolaitan "helps" by ignoring the plain meaning and giving a "deeper" meaning. Nicolaitan spiritualizing is mostly just flights of fancy.

A second tactic to make the Bible seem more difficult to understand is education. Nicolaitans use it like a hammer to keep believers in line. Education must mean they know more about the Word, right? So they tell you, "Sit down and shut up because you don't know the original languages." Or they'll say you haven't studied all of the in-depth systematic theologies, which proves you are an ignoramus. Other slap-downs are that you haven't sold as many books, you don't make as much money, and you don't have a mega-Church. Therefore, you are not possibly qualified to determine meaning. You must listen to them and them alone. Yeah, well, it seems the more education one gets in our modern age the dumber you tend to become. Nicolaitans major in pride and philosophies of men, not the Bible, which dumbs down their curriculum pretty quick.

Nicolaitans want to be the source for guidance instead of The Word. They have a nice position with people hanging on their every ear-tickling word, and their authority with many is unquestioned. They have learned to give their flock what it wants, meaning to feed the flesh. It gives them control over you. Position, authority and pride are the three main fertilizers that cause Nicolaitan weeds to sprout up all over the place (Matthew 13). Sadly, many people are okay with this because they hear what they want to hear from these teachers. They think it relieves them of responsibility, but it really doesn't. So, unlike the Ephesians, Church-goers are not fighting back (Revelation 2:2).

Manipulate Emotions. As I discussed before, another Nicolaitan tactic is to use "love" a lot. Their version of love however is feelings oriented instead of anchoring in God's truth and obedience. Love rejoices in the truth (1 Corinthians 13:6) and God's Word is truth. Sentiment on the other hand results in being "tossed to and fro by the waves and carried about by every wind of doctrine" (Ephesians 4:14). Truth is not very popular, and in place of truth, the Nicolaitan focuses on emotion. What one feels about Jesus or God's Word (same thing) is more important than what the

Word actually says. Nicolaitan love lets people do harmful things such as kill babies even after they are born, choose alternate lifestyles or observe the Day of the Dead. God's love is real in that He gives us instructions for avoiding things that hurt us, like a parent who won't let a child play on the freeway. Teaching love as sentiment minus truth confuses the issues and contributes to what Andy Stanley says of the Church.

> Many people see Christianity as anti-intellectual, overly simplistic, and easily discredited. For decades, college professors with biases against religion have found Christian freshmen easy targets. [4]

My response to Andy is, "It isn't because of the Bible. It's because of all the dippy extra-biblical Nicolaitan dogma, and the refusal to teach and observe the Bible consistently. It is your false teaching on love and many other issues that is anti-intellectual, overly simplistic and easily discredited. Not the Bible."

I'm a passionate person. When I was younger and, um, less restrained, I prayed for help to be more Spirit controlled. I asked that He would help guide my passion, but not to take it away from me. Passion is a good emotion, and emotions are a part of how God put us together. Nicolaitan Church teachings sure didn't help me. They steered me away from the parts of the Bible that really do help, and substituted with sentiment alone. I want my passion to be Spirit-controlled as Jesus directs, and I think He is answering my prayer by taking in and doing all of His Word.

Nicolaitan tactics depend on emotion alone quite a bit. They "acquire the fire" then don't know what to do with it, except maybe burn others. It's considered wonderful if a teacher or speaker or writer of articles and books connects with listeners or readers on an emotional level. It is good to connect to our Messiah, God and savior with emotion. But emotions alone are not enough.

---

[4] http://www.foxnews.com/opinion/2018/09/23/five-reasons-people-leave-church.html. Online Fox News Opinion article 9/23/18.

Connecting emotionally all by itself, without the Spirit or the Word, is the cause of a lot of sin and grief. We need the balance to our emotions that God's Word brings. Sowing emotions by themselves generally leads to a harvest of heartache.

Cling to Tradition. Emotion plays a big part in Nicolaitan tactics in the area of Church traditions. Christmas for instance has a very deep well of emotion for many because from all the way back in childhood we got presents, pretty lights and trees, and usually family and good food. That sort of stuff builds a lot of emotional attachment to the Church. Halloween is another emotional tradition case in point. It seems harmless for kids to dress up, go around collecting sweets for an evening and then fall into a sugar coma for a couple of weeks. Catholics say something like "give us a child for a while and he'll stay in the Church for life." This is because of the traditions and all the emotion that goes into them. They hook us on emotional traditions in order to give us strong reasons to stay in their fold.

Much of the Church traditions were part of my life too, and they were tough to give up. I didn't have quite the family life I wanted in childhood so I looked forward to establishing it in my marriage, which we did. Then I had to change things when I discovered whole Bible Christianity. My teenage kids had a tough time also, because we had done a good job with Church doctrine and tradition as they were growing up. But as I absorbed the shock of a whole Bible faith, I had to ask myself, "Is a little harmless paganism okay?" The Bible said no. A little paganism opens the door to a lot of paganism and clouds the love of God in the Word. To make it more clear, I ask the question this way: "Is a little hate okay with God?" Happily, my family saw the light too.

Nicolaitans appeal to "Church fathers," which are those shepherds from around two to four hundred years or so after Jesus went up into the clouds, to shore up their authority and teaching claims. They believe that the father's teachings couldn't be wrong because they were fairly close to the time of Jesus and the apostles.

But "old" or "close" doesn't mean "biblical." There's a large time gap between the apostles and the Church fathers, and the Bible doesn't confirm most of their writings unless the words are twisted or spiritualized to fit. Still, the father's traditions are nearly sacred.

There was lots of turmoil in the centuries after the apostles, with people arguing back and forth about doctrine, especially once the Church started to appear. At least seven Church councils were held in Constantinople (modern Istanbul) and surrounding areas, starting with the first at Nicea (a suburb) in 325 A. D. when the Church was officially born. Six more were held every so often for about 400 years after that. One of them was in Ephesus, home of the Nicolaitans. Those Church councils form a large part of the foundation doctrine and traditions of the Church. All of the councils were under the supervision, or ownership, of the Roman Empire. Church father teachings come mostly from those councils. No matter how old the teachings are or how close they are to the apostles, they didn't come from the Bible.

Protect the Tower. A huge, well dug-in tradition is the existence of the Church itself. The overriding goal of a Nicolaitan is to build and preserve this "new thing." Since man created the Church, and it is not in the Bible, it takes every tactic they can think of to prop it up. Those who believe in the Church strive their utmost to maintain this unbiblical construct, such as Jan Markell of Olive Tree Ministries who says, "Christ died for His Church."[5] He didn't die for the Church, Jan. He died to pay for our sin.

The tower of Babel was supposed to keep the people of the world united without God. In like manner, man created the Church tower to have an identity separate from Israel. Brick by brick Nicolaitans built this tower over the centuries from many philosophies of men (Colossians 2:8) which we'll talk about in the next chapter. It is spooky how much the Church tower resembles

---

[5] Presentation from a Dave Reagan prophecy conference included in a Compass International email of 11/15/2018.

the Tower of Babel and how fiercely they defend it. As I mentioned previously, many Nicolaitans will refer to the "Church fathers," and ask if they could all be wrong, whenever anyone questions the Church. As if it wasn't possible for a bunch of men to be wrong. Of course they could be wrong. Is everyone right all the time? Are men perfect? Those are rhetorical questions by the way.

Some Nicolaitans get close to realizing what is wrong in the Church. Randy White for instance has a presentation where he asks, "Where Have All The Pastors Gone?" lamenting "pastors who preach in a way to fill pews, not teach hard Bible truths."[6] But so far, Nicolaitans keep misidentifying solutions because they're blind to the false construct of the Church tower. They protect it instead of tearing it down. Jason F. Wright says that Church is the answer to all your problems.[7] No, Jason, the Church isn't the answer. The Word of God is the answer. He says Church is the place to go to "immerse yourself in the greatest truth ever told." It might be, if Jesus was actually in the Church. But He's not there because His Word is largely absent. The Church is a corrupt organization building a tower "with its top in the heavens" (Genesis 11:4) using fired bricks of theology and bitumen mortar philosophies of men (Genesis 11:3) to make a name.

Jan Markell almost gets to the truth in her previously mentioned conference when she says there is a big problem in the Church. But then she takes a left turn when she says it's because Churches are not teaching dispensationalism! Sorry Jan. The problem isn't that Churches are not teaching some false, made-up philosophy of men. It's that there is no Church in the Bible. They aren't teaching and living the Bible in the first place, and dispensationalism itself has helped to displace many good Bible teachings. I used to teach it, so I know whereof I speak.

---

[6] Compass International eNews email 12/11/2018 advertising a Steeling the Mind Bible Conference for February 16, 2019.
[7] Opinion editorial on foxnews.com 11/17/18 "Church is For Sinners https://www.foxnews.com/opinion/is-church-for-sinners.

Plausible Arguments. Speaking of dispensationalism, Nicolaitans have gone to great lengths creating philosophical mortar to hold together the bricks in their Tower of Babel. Almost every major doctrine, from amillenialism to dispensationalism and from Arminianism to Calvinism, developed pretty much either with the Church as the center or to shore up their Tower. The tactic is to keep us arguing about philosophies of men in order to distract from what God tells us to do, or to explain away parts of His Word like the Law. I don't have enough space to describe each doctrine completely, but a few summaries aren't too much to tackle here. You can review them yourself to see just how much they are all "Church" centered, and how much we can really do without them if we just read and follow the whole Bible.

Dispensationalism is a philosophy of men that imagines seven ages in the Bible. In each age, they suppose God deals with people differently than in other ages. For instance, the age when Israel was "under" the Law of Moses is the "Age of Law." The "Church age" or "Age of Grace" is the time after Jesus when the Law is eliminated and we have grace instead. I used to be heavy into this, learning from a seven-volume systematic theology book series, written by the founder of Dallas Theological Seminary Lewis Sperry Chafer. Can you believe it? Seven books to learn a false doctrine and teach it. That is, I taught it until I actually read the whole Bible and started following it. Well, that study wasn't a complete waste of time. There is a lot of truth in those books, and it was good training for eventually pinning down some Nicolaitan teachings. Dispensationalism is useless because it tries to account for a Church that isn't in the Bible, it obscures rather than clarifies Bible teachings, and it doesn't help me with daily life at all.

Amillenialism (literally "no millennium kingdom") says the Church will eventually save the world. Again, this popped up because there's nothing in the Bible about the Church. People are confused because they think the Church is the body of Christ, and since Jesus is King of Kings, his body (falsely identified as the

Church) must be powerful (the gates of hell cannot prevail) too. It is similar to universalism (the teaching that there is no hell), meaning that everyone will eventually be saved. This is another plausible argument only very loosely based on some of the Word.

Calvinism and Arminianism are two sides of a debate about salvation. Subjects include getting it, losing it, and keeping it. This complicated debate would go away in a heartbeat if people just did what God said. Are you saved? Then do what God says. How am I saved? Do what God says. Can I decide not to be saved? Perhaps you weren't saved in the first place because Jesus tells us to be patient and persevere in doing what God says. Once I'm saved, am I always saved? I'll tell you what - do what God says, keep doing what God says, and you'll be able to face the Father in the end at the side of the Messiah. Your salvation is in His hands. See what I mean? The life of a believer revolves around trusting a loving, merciful God and doing what He commands. Even repentance is a command to be followed (Acts 17:30).

> Ecclesiastes 12:11–13, ESV (parenthesis added). The words of the wise are like goads (a poke or a smack to get moving), and like nails firmly fixed are the collected sayings; they are given by one Shepherd. My son, beware of anything beyond these. Of making many books there is no end, and much study is a weariness of the flesh. The end of the matter; all has been heard. Fear God and keep his commandments, for this is the whole duty of man.

Misuse Words. Nicolaitans have deceptive tactics because they use a lot of words and concepts lifted directly from the Bible, but they make them mean different things than a plain reading gives us. All while claiming they are teaching the plain meaning! They change definitions so they can seem to be teaching biblically, when they are really leading away from His living oracles.

Glaring examples are the Old/New Testament labels. The old covenant or testament to them is the books before the new covenant. The new covenant is the New Testament. This sounds good, until we read the Bible and find the actual new covenant, highlighted by Jeremiah and Ezekiel 600 years before Jesus.

> Jeremiah 31:31–34, ESV. "Behold, the days are coming, declares the LORD, when I will make a new covenant with the house of Israel and the house of Judah, not like the covenant that I made with their fathers on the day when I took them by the hand to bring them out of the land of Egypt, my covenant that they broke, though I was their husband, declares the LORD. For this is the covenant that I will make with the house of Israel after those days, declares the LORD: I will put my law within them, and I will write it on their hearts. And I will be their God, and they shall be my people. And no longer shall each one teach his neighbor and each his brother, saying, 'Know the LORD,' for they shall all know me, from the least of them to the greatest, declares the LORD. For I will forgive their iniquity, and I will remember their sin no more."

When Jesus spoke of "this cup that is poured out for you is the new covenant in my blood" (Luke 22:20) there was no explanation because He didn't need to explain. Everyone knew what He was talking about. It had been expected and taught for hundreds of years. The New Covenant is the "Law within them, and I will write it on their hearts." It's between Israel, God and Judah. Gentiles are "brought near" (Ephesians 2:13) or "grafted in" (Romans 9-11) and are the "other sheep not of this fold" (John 10:16). What is new is the heart. Ezekiel, who lived about the same time as Jeremiah, fills in details about the new heart of flesh.

> Ezekiel 11:19–20, ESV. And I will give them one heart, and a new spirit I will put within them. I will remove the heart of stone from their flesh and give them a heart of flesh, that they may walk in my statutes and keep my rules and obey them. And they shall be my people, and I will be their God.

> Ezekiel 36:26–27, ESV. And I will give you a new heart, and a new spirit I will put within you. And I will remove the heart of stone from your flesh and give you a heart of flesh. And I

will put my Spirit within you, and cause you to walk in my
statutes and be careful to obey my rules.

The plain meaning is obvious. Believers gain a new heart
of flesh written with the Law, by the Spirit, causing us to walk in
God's commands. Nicolaitans instead reduce the Law to "historical
context and inspiration" in the words of Andy Stanley. Then they
change the new covenant into some sort of nebulous, feelings
oriented "testament" (KJV) which makes very few demands for
righteous living based on the Bible.

This way they can do what is right in their own eyes in the
name of a love that is emotion only. When meaning is divorced
from the Bible text, they can tickle ears and lead where they want.
Proselytes have to go to them for instruction rather than the Bible.
See how that works? It is a neat transfer of authority from the
Bible to the Nicolaitan. And they are the ones who tell you what
Christian behavior is and what it isn't.

A beautiful thing about the New Covenant is that it didn't
require changing or eliminating the bulk of the Old Covenant. The
only modification was in the priesthood, because Jesus as our high
priest is from Judah, not Levi. What is new about the New
Covenant is the heart. The New Covenant shows the brilliance of
God in keeping the Old, written on stone, yet giving it a new
approach, one it should've always had. The new approach was in
writing the Old Covenant on a new heart of flesh. The New
Covenant in tandem with the Old kept the unchanging nature of
God's Word and invigorated it. It's a continuous message of life
and love from a longsuffering, patient Father. The blood of Jesus
removed the Pharisee's dusty, old, incapacitating yoke of bondage
of their oral laws, rulings and traditions from the Law and filled it
back full of love. Now the Nicolaitan Church has drained the life
and loaded up His Word again with their own oral laws.

Another glaring example of word misuse is to divide the
Law into civil, ceremonial and moral sections; as if everything

God says isn't moral. Have you ever wondered why only the external parts of the Law were terminated in Church theology? You know, the ones that would make believers look like Jews? Could it be an excuse to avoid looking like a Jew? Like maybe to avoid a Roman tax? Isn't it also suspicious that the "ceremonial" tithe made it past the cross when the other ceremonial parts didn't?

God does not use these labels and they aren't in the Bible as such. Dividing this way makes cherry-picking the Word into an art form. The Nicolaitan puts the disliked portion of the living oracles into one of those categories and then ignores it. This is problem enough, but a bigger problem comes in when people use the labels to excuse any behavior and think to remain in God's Kingdom.

> Revelation 21:8, ESV. But as for the cowardly, the faithless, the detestable, as for murderers, the sexually immoral, sorcerers, idolaters, and all liars, their portion will be in the lake that burns with fire and sulfur, which is the second death."

When we slice and dice God's Word we are actually slicing and dicing Jesus. That's a bit of a mystical thought, I know, but He is the Living Word. He modeled obedience to God's Word for us in every way, His will was to do the Father's will, and He followed every word from God without exception. Cutting out parts of the Word is like cutting out parts of Jesus. I don't want just part, I want the whole thing. I want all of the Bread of Life.

Speak for Jesus. Speaking for Jesus is fine, if you speak the words of Jesus as He meant them. This generally means taking His words in their plain, easy to understand meaning and completeness. Speaking for Jesus is a dangerous thing, but so many Nicolaitans take it so lightly. Jesus tells us plainly, for instance, that we are to go forth, make disciples, teach them to obey all He commanded, and baptize them in the name of the Father, Son and Holy Spirit (Matthew 28:19-20). The Nicolaitan has the nerve to claim He didn't say that. Instead, they say what Jesus really meant was the complete opposite of what is written!

When Jesus says, "I came not to abolish but to fulfill" (the Law and the Prophets) the Nicolaitan will say that "fulfill" means the same thing as "abolish" or "terminate." This doesn't make any sense. Did Jesus really say, "I came not to abolish but to abolish?" Did He really say He was going to abolish the prophets along with the Law? Obviously, in the plain reading, fulfill would be something opposite of abolish.

We get clues as to what He means when He goes on to explain that "until heaven and earth pass away, not an iota, not a dot, will pass from the Law until all is accomplished." On the heels of that statement He then says, "Therefore whoever relaxes one of the least of these commandments and teaches others to do the same will be called least in the kingdom of heaven." If you look it up, fulfill means something like "establish" or "confirm" or even like filling a cup before handing it to someone. It seems plain that Jesus filled back up His Law full of love and then handed it to believers.

No Questions. Nicolaitans do not like questions, especially when you challenge their teachings using the Word. They will either dodge them or give fanciful answers with no references from Scripture. Or hang up on you. They avoid questions, ignore Scripture, use circular reasoning and apply faulty logic to make it look like they are answering when they aren't. The true teacher rightly divides the Word, and isn't afraid of challenges. "Always be prepared to make a defense to anyone who asks you for a reason for the hope that is in you" (1 Peter 3:15, my paraphrase). See the email exchange at the end of the book for a typical dead-end conversation with a Nicolaitan who will not answer questions.

Ecclesiastes 10:2, ESV. A wise man's heart inclines him to the right, but a fool's heart to the left.

Disconnect. An ancient tactic Nicolaitans use all the time is to disconnect parts of the Bible from each other. They separate

Israel from believers or divide the Bible into different ages. New Testament for Christians, Old Testament for Jews. But God's Word is one continuous message to one body as Paul said in Ephesians 4:4. It isn't broken up, God never has to re-figure a plan, and He is never out-guessed. Nicolaitans, on the other hand, constantly have to come up with deceptive answers to the plain teaching of the Word. If we read it as one faith to one body, His Word is unified.

Control Salvation. Controlling access to salvation is another tactic of the Nicolaitans. Jewish Nicolaitans thought you had to become a Jew, because in many of the rabbi's interpretations all Jews are saved. Circumcision was needed, and you have to follow the rabbi's rulings (not just Torah). This is why the apostles had a meeting in Acts 15. The outcome of that meeting was that salvation for all is by grace through faith, as it had always been. Believers learn how to live because Moses is taught in the synagogue every Sabbath (Acts 15:21). Paul was playing off of this idea when he explains salvation is "through faith" and "all Israel will be saved" (all believers - Romans 11:20, 26). This is also why the mob went nuts when Paul told them he was sent to the Gentiles. He was saying Gentiles were included in the kingdom (Acts 22:19-22), and the Jews thought salvation was only for Jews.

Catholic Nicolaitans control salvation by cutting people off from their freaky Holy Communion and the confessional. In their interpretation (which is way outside the Bible), only people who eat the "body" and drink the "blood" of Christ are saved. Their version of body and blood, however, is a wafer and wine which they think actually becomes the body and blood of Christ through their communion ceremony. It doesn't have anything to do with obedience, which is what Jesus was trying to say in John 6:53-58.

Protestants control access to salvation by chasing people away from the Bible, specifically the Law (which they misclassify as "works") and towards a mystical "acceptance" of Christ. Throw in perhaps a "sinner's prayer" or going down front at a stadium shindig, and sometimes baptism. Whatever you do, you can't follow His Law. Like the Holy Communion, this acceptance of Jesus also has nothing to do with obedience. It seems to mean that if you go to church and put some money in the plate, look like them, dress like them, and talk like them then you must be saved (I want to be a clone). Just make sure to put that tithe in the plate.

All of these Nicolaitans set up fictitious salvation methods and then control access by various extra-biblical measurements and theology. The Bible says on the other hand that people have direct access to God and all they have to do is repent. Stop going their own way and go God's way. It really is that simple.

Hate Israel. A Nicolaitan gives himself away immediately if he hates Israel. Hate for Israel comes in different forms and mixtures. The Church in general uses a hateful teaching called Replacement Theology to say that the Church has replaced Israel. The theory is that since the Jews crucified Jesus, they lost their status as God's favorite. According to this theory, Israel wouldn't obey God so He created the Church. Some replacement believers such as dispensationalists still claim to love Israel; they just relegate them to second-class citizens and give them all the curses of the Bible. They believe that one purpose of the Tribulation is to cleanse and purge Israel to bring them into His kingdom. I searched and I can't find this in the Bible anywhere.

A more overt form of Israel hating is in the boycott-divest-sanction (BDS) movement. BDS punishes Israel by bullying people to avoid investing money in anything connected with Israel. BDS Nicolaitans claim to want Israel to end what it calls "apartheid and colonialism" but really, they just hate Israel. The deceiver hates Israel too so these people are obviously his children, not God's. No matter how one is to dress this up, it is still simply Israel-hating. One cannot hate Israel and at the same time be a believer. They just do not go together biblically at all. In my opinion, and I think the Word backs it up, we cannot claim to follow God while hating the "apple of His eye" (Zechariah 2:8).

Israel may not be doing everything right in God's eyes. Their leaders really did do a terrible thing by turning Jesus over to the Romans and insisting with false allegations that He be executed. In modern times, they still haven't squared things away with God as a nation. I get it. God knows all that and loves them anyway. He loves us too even if we screw up.

If you want to have fun with BDS then use it on Muslims. Islam is a hate-filled religion worshipping a false god of the moon, and adherents relentlessly attack any nation not in line with them. Mosques are filled with Nicolaitans. Almost every war or conflict in the world today involves Muslims. Israel has a democratic government which allows even Muslims a voice. Muslims on the other hand have tyrannical, fascist governments. Israel got a tiny sliver of desert and is turning it into a garden that might rival Eden, with God's blessing. Muslims have a huge amount of land and wealth from oil yet still import most of their food. Israel is a peaceful nation thriving in the midst of millions who hate them. Everywhere Muslims go, they leave death and destruction in their wake. If you want to boycott someone, pick a Muslim nation.

Divide Wrongly. A favorite tactic of a Nicolaitan is wrongly dividing the Word. One way they do this is by calling opponents "divisive." Divisive can be a good thing, or it can be bad. Paul tells us in 1 Corinthians 11:19 that "there must be factions among you in order that those who are genuine among you may be recognized." Jesus said "Do you think that I have come to give peace on earth? No, I tell you, but rather division" (Luke 12:51) and again in Matthew 10:34, "Do not think that I have come to bring peace to the earth. I have not come to bring peace, but a sword." John tells us "there was division among the people over him" in John 7:43. So apparently divisive is not such a bad thing, if it is over the Word.

This of course doesn't excuse those who stir up strife and division over things that are not in the Word. There are several warnings about divisive people such as Titus 3:10. But this type of division is from those whom Jude describes as "...scoffers, following their own ungodly passions. It is these who cause divisions, worldly people, devoid of the Spirit." This is for people like the Nicolaitans. It is not from people who want to stick to God's Word and defend it against those who would destroy it.

Dividing is also an old name for handling or discerning the Word of Truth as Paul says in 2 Timothy 2:15. It is the opposite of "irreverent babble." Some Nicolaitans think that we can only rightly divide the Word if we understand their extra-biblical babble, I mean doctrine, first. I'm here to tell you that is not the case. God communicated His plan and instructions to us in plain language. The main impediment to understanding is not the Church dogma but our willingness to accept His Words and do them. Rightly dividing also means "right doing." We can't say we believe God and refuse to do what He says, now, can we?

If we are asking legitimate questions about the Word, that can be a divisive thing but not a bad divisive thing. "The Word of God is living and active, sharper than any two-edged sword, piercing to the division of soul and spirit, of joints and of marrow, and discerning the thoughts and intentions of the heart" (Hebrews 4:12). If we are clarifying a teaching that is supposed to be from the Word by the Word, then the heart of the Nicolaitan is revealed. Is it soft, humble and responsive to every word God speaks? Or is it as hard as stone tablets?

6 What They Teach

John 5:46, ESV. For if you believed Moses, you would believe me; for he wrote of me.

In the last chapter, we looked at how the Nicolaitans teach. In this chapter, we will look at what they teach. I'm calling their teaching by the same name Paul used: philosophies of men. One dictionary definition of philosophy that I think the best is "a search for a general understanding of values and reality by chiefly speculative rather than observational means." The philosophies of men (Colossians 2:8) in relation to the Bible are speculative (from their own minds) instead of observational (what the Bible says). In other words, Nicolaitans just make it up. Evolution is a prime example. There is zero evidence for it. So-called scientists just make it up. It sneaks into the Church because Church teachings are so lacking in God's Word and so full of holes that some have tried desperately to plug them with godless philosophies of men.

There are a number of places in the Bible God tells us different ways that men supersede, cover over, deliberately misunderstand, or otherwise modify His Word. As we see with Colossians 2, for instance, philosophies of men interfere with the celebration of God's holidays, promote extra-biblical practices such as forbidding marriage or living like a monk, and prevent believers from obtaining "all the riches of full assurance of understanding and the knowledge of God's mystery, which is Christ." In verse 5 Paul says to avoid the delusion of plausible arguments blocking us from the "riches of God's mystery Christ in whom are hidden all the treasures of wisdom and knowledge." In verse 8, Paul warns us not to be "taken captive by philosophy and empty deceit, according to human tradition, according to the elemental spirits of the world and not according to Christ."

As you are reading, you might be wondering, as I have, about the reason so many Church philosophies seem to be anti-law.

My conclusion is it is because the Bible teaches us to do God's Law in many different ways, but our nature is to dodge every one.

I tried in this chapter to group philosophies under general headings because I couldn't cover every philosophy. There are so many I would have to write a bunch of books to hold them. Hopefully I've put enough in this book to guide you in spotting and avoiding them. But this book is just a helping hand; the real help comes from reading and doing all of His glorious living oracles.

The Appearance of Wisdom. All false teachers, including the Nicolaitans, use philosophies of men to look good. But looks can be deceiving. Paul lists several specific philosophies such as asceticism (the belief that material things cause sin and so should be avoided), worship of angels (the word means "messengers;" this includes saints, the Virgin Mary, and so on), visions (any mysterious sight that takes us away from the Word), a sensuous mind (sexual immorality), and not holding fast the Head of the body (denying the deity of Jesus, Colossians 2:9; 1 John 2:22-23).

"Do not handle, Do not taste, Do not touch" in Colossians 2:21 is directly related to the asceticism described in 2:18 (such as being a vegan) and has nothing to do with God's Laws. Paul says that these teachings look good ("have an appearance of wisdom" from verse 2:23) and promote self-made religion and asceticism and severity to the body, but are of no value in stopping the indulgence of the flesh. In other words, these practices look good but don't work spiritually. The following is a list of the false teachings common to Nicolaitans and other false teachers.

1. Asceticism - laboring in false humility.
2. Worship of angels (messengers) when every actual messenger from God tells people not to.
3. Visions - any mysterious sight or dream that takes us away from the Word.
4. Sensuous mind - the opposite of asceticism; sexual immorality, gluttony, fastidious.
5. Denying the deity or Messiah-ship of Jesus.

6. Self-made religion - creating laws outside of the Bible.
7. Different doctrine than what is written (1 Corinthians 4:6).
8. Myths; irreverent, silly (1 Timothy 1:4, 4:7), Jewish (Titus 1:14).
9. Endless genealogies (1 Timothy 1:4), genealogies (Titus 3:9), including Hebrew roots teachings.
10. Foolish controversies, dissensions (Titus 3:9).
11. Quarrels about law (little L) otherwise known as a lawyer.
12. Vain discussion; teaching leading nowhere or away from the Word; philosophy, empty deceit.
13. Devoting themselves to deceitful spirits and teachings of demons.
14. Forbid marriage.
15. Stirs up division (Titus 3:10) away from the Bible.
16. Dietary restrictions outside of the Bible.
17. Desiring to be teachers of the Law without understanding. Includes those who teach against the Law with the following philosophies and others like them:
    a. The Law was given to condemn.
    b. The Church replaced Israel.
    c. The Law is only for Jews.
    d. Moses brought condemnation; Jesus, grace.
    e. The indwelling of the Spirit began at Pentecost.
    f. Paul was all things to all men: ignored the Law.
    g. Jesus broke the Sabbath.
    h. The Law is a burden/death/curse/slavery.
    i. The Law was fulfilled (partially terminated).
    j. The Law is not spiritual.
    k. Jesus' Law replaced the Law of Moses.
    l. The Church has the Spirit, doesn't need the letter.

There are many other false teachings, but this gives us an idea of the many ways Nicolaitan teachings have the appearance of wisdom. They look like they are from God's Word but are not God's Word. Wolves in sheep's clothing use some language from the Bible to disguise the fact they are leading away from God's Word, and so deny the flock the blessings of it.

> Jeremiah 23:28–29, ESV. Let the prophet who has a dream tell the dream, but let him who has my word speak my word faithfully. What has straw in common with wheat? declares the LORD. Is not my word like fire, declares the LORD, and like a hammer that breaks the rock in pieces?

Asceticism in Colossians means something like "voluntary humility." Our English word comes from a Greek adjective (transliterated *asketikos*) meaning "laborious." Put them together and you have the idea of laboring to be humble, usually by denial of pleasure or comfort. Like monks, or people who crucify themselves. It is a sneaky philosophy because we are all prone to it (think fasting), and there are some advantages in helping us avoid some unhealthy behavior. The problem comes in when we develop a law apart from the Bible which we then impose on others.

For instance, many Baptists dislike dancing because they deem it "fleshly" or catering to the flesh. This is fine. If you don't want to dance then don't. But when you impose it on others, then it becomes "an appearance of wisdom" but has "no value in stopping the indulgence of the flesh" (Colossians 2:23). It's an "oral law;" a burdensome yoke. Some Churches ban musical instruments, contrary to their use in the Bible. Smoking is another no-no for many, and it is good to avoid it I think. But as an ascetic principle, non-smoking doesn't really work to inspire spiritual growth.

The key is to fill up with God's Word and God's practices such as Sabbath and diet. These are different from philosophies of men in that God gives them. So when we do them in love and the Spirit they work to impart blessings pressed down and overflowing. A big part of filling up is humbly submitting to every Word. We change from a take-it-or-leave-it attitude to one of laying down our life. His Word makes good changes in us.

We can pat ourselves on the back that we don't worship angels, but what about being enamored of a priest or pastor? Do we elevate a man to a position of worship by listening to him instead of the Bible? In many instances this is exactly what happens. How about visions? I've been told a few times that to make spiritual progress I needed a "vision of the resurrected Christ." Ray Bentley of Calvary Chapel tried to get us one time to "visualize the throne room and Jesus sitting on the throne." Visions are quite common in the Church but they mostly lead away from the Word, not toward it. Endless genealogies can be seen in certain Churches or synagogues with the fascination of Hebrew ancestry, Hebrew Roots teachings, or the desire for Hebrew originals for the gospels. Foolish controversies such as those over Bible codes, tongues or the rapture abound.

The part about desiring to be teachers of the Law goes both ways: those that teach against it and those who teach for it. Within both of these groups, there are extremes of thinking. Those that teach against the Law are unscriptural but they still come up with all sorts of their own laws as the Pharisees did. I remember calling a Pentecostal Holiness Church and the pastor read off a list of all the laws they had. There were laws like women can't wear makeup and the genders can't swim together. At the same time, there weren't many of God's Laws on the list. Strange how God's laws are not acceptable but man's are. Those that teach for the Law are scriptural as long as they teach the Word. But there are also some who, like the Pharisees, come up with all kinds of extra laws that are supposed to be Bible based and are not. It's obvious that extremes are common in people who cut loose from God's Law, such as the part about not adding to or subtracting from it (Deuteronomy 4:2, 12:32; Ecclesiastes 3:14).

Those twelve statements under number 17 on the list of false teachings are typical of the many, many anti-law teachings of the Nicolaitans. Paul warned Timothy (1 Timothy 1) about these types of false teachers. False teachers were already present in the Ephesian assembly Timothy was leading, and they had swerved from love. A few decades later, they became the Nicolaitans. Many Nicolaitans have swerved away from love issuing from a pure heart, good conscience and sincere faith. So they wander into vain discussion, desiring to be teachers of the Law without understanding either what they are saying or the things about which they make confident assertions (1 Timothy 1:6-7 my paraphrase). False shepherds speak against God's wonderful living oracles in so many ways one has to wonder, why? The answer is in the letter to the Ephesians in Revelation 2. Jesus says "you have abandoned the love you had at first." It's the same indictment given by Paul perhaps 30 or so years earlier. When we wander away from the Law, we wander away from truth and love.

Cutting ourselves loose from the anchor of the Word we go in all sorts of crazy, Nicolaitan directions. If we just stick with the plain, written meaning (1 Corinthians 4:6) I don't think we can go wrong. If Jesus said something specific, let's follow what He says. If He doesn't make a law, we should leave it alone. We seem to have trouble enough doing the few instructions God gave us.

Blinding Faith. One of the many ways these false teachings impact the believer is in blinding our faith. As I explained briefly before, the Nicolaitan places him or herself between the Bible and the believer, and like a translator from hell explains the Bible in such a way that we can't just accept the plain meaning. We have to consult with the Nicolaitan in order to understand and apply the Word. Since the Nicolaitan has very little basis in the Word for his teachings, we get to where we can't make sense of the Bible on our own. This is why most Christians are tagged with the "blind faith" label - because we are reduced to explaining our beliefs with "we just have to take it on faith." We don't know how to explain what we believe from the Bible because we are not taught the Bible. We are just taught dogma from a teacher who might be a nice guy but doesn't know or follow the Bible himself.

In an article titled "Rightly Dividing the Word" in Compass Communiqué, Issue #3 in 2018, Bill Perkins writes, "If you're not a dispensationalist, you've got big problems regarding how you understand your Bible!" So according to Bill, you can't just read the Bible and figure out what it says. You have to know the extra-biblical doctrine of dispensationalism first. That doctrine isn't in the Bible, so you have to go to a Nicolaitan to find out what it is. If you read the Bible according to the doctrine, you have to break the Word into unrelated pieces and fit the pieces into different parts of the theology. Like many Nicolaitans, Bill strains hard to make the Bible fit his Church theology. Of course, he thinks he is "rightly dividing the word." No wonder there's a veil on believers!

Paul tells us to take the blinding veil off in 2 Corinthians 3:12-18. Turn to Jesus and remove the veil from our hearts. Then when we read Moses, we can see Jesus in the Laws He gave and there is freedom. "We all, with unveiled face, beholding the glory of the Lord, are being transformed into the same image from one degree of glory to another. For this comes from the Lord who is the Spirit." Believers turn to the Lord, the veil is removed, and then we see. When Moses is read (and practiced) we are transformed.

If we can't understand the Bible, that means we haven't turned to Jesus. Perhaps instead of Jesus, we are turning to Church. Church dogma and Nicolaitan teaching cause "big problems regarding how we understand the Bible."

Sandy Foundations. The philosophies of men taught by the Nicolaitans use only part of the Bible, mainly to give some authority to their false teachings. Like Jezebel grabbing authority by claiming to be a prophetess. So the foundation that believers are handed has many pieces missing, like concrete that is missing half of the cement. All we have left is not very solid. We try to construct our lives on this foundation but it gives way beneath us all too often. Even a light breeze causes whatever we're building to fall. As Jesus said, a house built on sand cannot endure a storm.

Have you ever wondered why a change of pastors causes many Churches to fall apart? It's due to a sandy foundation, built on the pastor's speaking style instead of the Word. Hundreds of pastors over the years have woken up to find they have lost their faith. Some are now atheists. I wish I could reassure them that they probably didn't lose faith in God; most just lost faith in the Church.

One of the big reasons that liberal, anti-God college professors find Christian freshman such an easy mark for destruction of their belief systems is, you guessed it, a sandy foundation. All they have is dogma in place of the Word. The real meaning and practice of family and the Body of Christ is missing (Ephesians 2:20); people have little defense for the world's attacks.

Sandy foundations also figure in when believers get married. I know from experience that churchgoers don't have the tools or the base on which to build a healthy, godly marriage. It's no wonder that so many of the marriages fail. It gets even worse when the pair tries to raise kids. They don't know what to do when things aren't working out according to the non-biblical books, and they can't really figure out the Bible because of the Nicolaitan teaching. Parents aren't any help because they got the same "orthodox" teaching from the Nicolaitans.

> Malachi 2:14–16 ESV. ...the LORD was witness between you and the wife of your youth, to whom you have been faithless, though she is your companion and your wife by covenant. Did he not make them one, with a portion of the Spirit in their union? And what was the one God seeking? Godly offspring. So guard yourselves in your spirit, and let none of you be faithless to the wife of your youth. "For the man who does not love his wife but divorces her, says the LORD, the God of Israel, covers his garment with violence, says the LORD of hosts. So guard yourselves in your spirit, and do not be faithless."

When Jesus said "everyone who hears these words of mine and does them" in the Sermon on the Mount (Matthew 7:24-27) there was no New Testament; it was written 30 or 40 years later. So was He talking about just the words in that Sermon? If I was there listening, and He converted me right at the moment of that sermon, did Jesus mean I only had this most recent Sermon on the Mount to go by? Or was He confirming the Old Testament and telling me to "hear" His first sermon too? I think it's clear that He was including the previous words of life and love He had given to His children at the first Sermon on the Mount (Sinai).

I've said many times the Nicolaitan Church has led the way into our current moral decay. Cherry-picking the Word and using only a few verses, along with maybe a psalm or two and the writings of Paul, is not enough for a strong foundation. God gave us the building blocks of His living oracles in written and walking (Jesus) forms, and all we have to do is take each instruction and lay it in place in our daily living. Then we become the walking Word, just like Jesus. Using the whole of His Word is a complete, rock-solid foundation on which we can construct our lives. With the Rock as a foundation, we can build those houses with gold, silver and precious stones that stand up to any storm or fire.

People try to touch God in different ways. Some use formal prayers, ceremonies and sacred songs. Others prefer a miraculous sign or two such as unknown languages, images revealed in food items or weeping statues. There are those who think separation from the rest of the world in monasteries or Amish communities is the way to go. God, however, looks to those who do what He says.

Isaiah 66:1–2, ESV (underline added). Thus says the LORD: "Heaven is my throne, and the earth is my footstool; what is the house that you would build for me, and what is the place of my rest? All these things my hand has made, and so all these things came to be, declares the LORD. But this is the one to whom I will look: he who is humble and contrite in spirit and trembles at my word.

Nicolaitans lead in the things that appeal to the flesh, such as emotion, and ignore most of the things that God says He wants. What God wants is a humble believer contrite in spirit trembling at His Word. This is boring to a lot of people, and just doesn't have the zing that we all would like to have. The Nicolaitans add the fleshly fireworks of signs and wonders such as healings or rock concerts to give it to us. Partly this is due to the demands of people who want to touch God through the senses. The other part is they just don't want to do what God says. We want to feel like we are doing what He says without really doing it.

Blame Shifting. Everybody, every person in history, every son or daughter of Adam, has a problem with any Word from God, especially the Law. When we fail to keep it, we shift the blame for it from ourselves to God. Nicolaitans raise "BS" to an art form. They call the Law "old" or "impossible to follow" or other such things as I said a few pages back. It is called The Law, but it is really just easy instructions from God for living. It is His Word to all His creation showing the way to life abundant. It is the gospel, as it says in Hebrews 4:2, because it is also "God with us."

When God gave The Law, it was because He was going to live with Israel. They were to be His kingdom on earth, and so He gave them a code, a constitution, or a series of instructions for living with Him. If God and Jesus are one, and I believe the Bible teaches that they are, and if no one has seen the Father but the Son and He has revealed Him (John 1:18), then Jesus gave The Law. Nicolaitans want you to believe that The Law is a bad thing; they call it "slavery" and "death" and say "no one can follow it." That makes blame shifting much easier. What Nicolaitans are really saying is it's God and His rules that are the problem.

There are those that claim that the Bible is full of errors. It is not, but even if it was, even if we couldn't trust it, The Law would still stand as a rule for living. If nothing else is accurate, if nothing could be counted on for truth, The Unchanging Law is there like a rock. What is so bad about it? The Law can be trusted. It is accurate and we can lean on it for living out His will. It is the heart of His will for creation. It is love. All of the theological arguments and disagreements can be eliminated or re-framed by observing The Law (remember, all of His Words). Just do it. At one time, it was written on stone. But the place where it really needs to be written is the heart of man.

Zechariah 7:8–12, ESV. And the word of the LORD came to Zechariah, saying, "Thus says the LORD of hosts, Render true judgments, show kindness and mercy to one another, do not oppress the widow, the fatherless, the sojourner, or the poor, and let none of you devise evil against another in your heart." But they refused to pay attention and turned a stubborn shoulder and stopped their ears that they might not hear. They made their hearts diamond-hard lest they should hear the law and the words that the LORD of hosts had sent by his Spirit through the former prophets. Therefore great anger came from the LORD of hosts.

Nicolaitans of all kinds, inside and outside the Church, miss that the essence of faith in God, of the Bible, of life abundant, is in following God's voice. Whether He walks with us in the Garden, speaks from Mount Sinai, teaches here incarnated or we read the Word on the page, His sheep listen to His voice and follow. A stranger we will not follow, but will flee from him because we don't know the voice of strangers. All the regulations, statutes, charges, commands, or whatever you want to call them, are His will for His children.

Jesus came to renew or confirm or fill up full The Law with love. That is what the deceiver really loathes about God, and loathing God's love is the key to all his tactics and strategy. He wants to hide or disguise or otherwise distract us from the love of God. The Law comes from love, it is shot through with love, it teaches us love, and the goal is love in Jesus. In a lot of ways the deceiver manages to cover over the love of God and make us believe that God really wants to find excuses to put us down or keep us down. Nicolaitans are his willing accomplices. They shift blame to God and so release people from doing what He says.

Blame shifting is an ancient art. It goes back to The Garden when the serpent told Eve, "He just doesn't want you to be like Him knowing good and evil" (Genesis 3:5 my paraphrase). Adam blamed "the woman that thou gavest me" and Eve blamed the serpent. Ultimately, they were blaming God. Nicolaitans want to protect their power and money, so they blame shift. They tell men that The Law is death, no one can follow it, or that God wasn't serious. It's all God's fault. They'll do anything to get our eyes off the living oracles of love and lead us in another direction.

The deceiver distracted Adam and Eve from following The Law. At that time, it was just a dietary command, which Nicolaitans call ceremonial. Modern, diamond-hearted Nicolaitans, following their father the deceiver, are working day and night to distract us from following the smallest command even now.

Immaturity. The philosophies of the Nicolaitans deny believers at least four benefits from the Word: maturity, fruit of the Spirit, touching God and abundant life. These all go together. Nicolaitans instead are mired in immature doctrines of Christ; as if they were endlessly watching reruns of "The Passion of Christ." Salvation is not the only thing; believers need to move on in the constant practice of sanctification. The writer of Hebrews says so.

> Hebrews 6:1–3, ESV. Therefore let us leave the elementary doctrine of Christ and go on to maturity, not laying again a foundation of repentance from dead works and of faith toward God, and of instruction about washings, the laying on of hands, the resurrection of the dead, and eternal judgment. And this we will do if God permits.

Churches are frozen in elementary doctrine of Christ. Repentance from dead works, faith toward God and so on is taught without letup. What does the writer of Hebrews say about that? "Let us leave the elementary doctrine of Christ and go on to maturity." Before Hebrews 6, the writer says there's more to life.

> Hebrews 5:11–14, ESV. About this we have much to say, and it is hard to explain, since you have become dull of hearing. For though by this time you ought to be teachers, you need someone to teach you again the basic principles of the oracles of God. You need milk, not solid food, for everyone who lives on milk is unskilled in the word of righteousness, since he is a child. But solid food is for the mature, for those who have

their powers of discernment trained by constant practice to distinguish good from evil.

I like milk, but I need more nutrition. I need solid food; all of His Word. Much of the Church is "dull of hearing" and "unskilled in the word of righteousness," and they "need someone to teach you again the basic principles of the oracles of God." What are the oracles of God but the Law, given by Jesus at Mount Sinai? Maturity comes from training our powers of discernment by constant practice. Believers distinguish good from evil using the oracles of God. The Law moves us on in maturity, not laying again (and again and again) an elementary foundation.

Nicolaitans repeatedly lay down the same immature teachings because they are pursuing personal agendas outside the Bible, instead of promoting maturity in the believer. What can we conclude but that they want believers to stay immature? Then we don't think for ourselves and find out we don't need the Nicolaitan!

Philippians 3:13–16, ESV. Brothers, I do not consider that I have made it my own. But one thing I do: forgetting what lies behind and straining forward to what lies ahead, I press on toward the goal for the prize of the upward call of God in Christ Jesus. Let those of us who are mature think this way, and if in anything you think otherwise, God will reveal that also to you. Only let us hold true to what we have attained.

Draining Jesus. It might not make much sense, but it seems that many in the Church were and are more in love with the idea of Jesus than with Jesus Himself. It's as if they believe in a Facebook Jesus. When Jesus says something they like, they give it a thumb up. If they dislike it, it gets a thumb down. If He says too many things they don't like, they block Him or even un-friend Him. In fact, we can say that the lopsided and incomplete Nicolaitan teachings about Jesus have turned Jesus into an idol.

That's right. The Jesus taught by Nicolaitans is an idol, mostly because they have drained Jesus of His own words and commands by trashing the "old covenant," and deliberately misinterpreting much of the rest of the Bible. Their Jesus is a hollow caricature; bled dry by the removal of His blood, which includes that so-called Old Covenant (John 6:53-58).

God's words are the body and blood of Jesus, who delighted to do the will of the Father in everything. The will of God is the food of Jesus as He says in John 4:34. He in turn is the bread from heaven which gives eternal life. The Words of the Father give Jesus form and purpose. Remove any of those words; rob them of meaning or reinterpret so you don't have to follow them, and by so much you reduce Jesus to an empty husk suitable only for worship at a distance.

On the other hand, if we take in all of His Words as if they were His body and blood, eat all of the bread of His life, we gain life more abundant. Jesus simply talks about worshipping God with all our heart, mind and strength (Deuteronomy 6:4-8; Mark 12:30; Luke 10:27) by following all of His commands. We don't have to be afraid of the Law. It is not an instrument of death. "It is your life" (Deuteronomy 32:45-47).

Cultural Appropriation. A well-developed philosophy of Nicolaitans is that Jesus made the Law harder with the Sermon on the Mount. The idea is that the Law was only external and Jesus got rid of external stuff. Compare this to the Greek (or pagan) idea that the material world is bad, and only the immaterial or spiritual things are good. With teachings like this, the Church has "appropriated" (it means to take, or make us of, without a right) Greek and pagan culture and pasted it on Jesus. First, they drain Him of the blood of His Word, then they spackle on some Greek funeral parlor makeup so their idol looks alive. It makes sense that the Church, heavily influenced by Roman and Greek culture from its beginning, would Hellenize their Jesus idol. They don't want Him to look or sound anything like the Jewish person He is. Present day churchgoers find a Hellenized Jesus comfortable, because we are so much like Greeks and Romans. The Church thinks it's a good thing Jesus used Greek ideas to free believers!

Jesus is Jewish in the purest sense because, just as God's Word gives Him form and purpose, it also gives Israel form and purpose. Greek philosophy is irreverent babble and lacks the love of God. God's love transforms our heart; the physical world is where we work it out. Salvation is not in merit for following some rules; it's in following His Words with a heart of love (Isaiah 1:12-17). His love and Law are not far from believers; they are in our hearts. Believers appropriate God's culture from His Word. Paul said something similar in Romans 10:6-13, using an ancient quote.

Deuteronomy 30:11–14, ESV. "For this commandment that I command you today is not too hard for you, neither is it far off. It is not in heaven, that you should say, 'Who will ascend to heaven for us and bring it to us, that we may hear it and do it?' Neither is it beyond the sea, that you should say, 'Who will go over the sea for us and bring it to us, that we may hear it and do it?' But the word is very near you. It is in your mouth and in your heart, so that you can do it.

The sacrifice of Jesus on the cross was always what made it possible for God to live in Israel, and for the animal sacrifices to work (such as they did) in the first place. If Jesus raised the bar, it was only because the Nicolaitan Pharisees had lowered it. They steered people away from the Law by their rulings, and modern Nicolaitans follow right in their footsteps.

Alone Faith. A hugely effective tactic Nicolaitans use on those who really don't read the Word (such as many Church-goers) is to characterize following the Law as "works." Works are said to be a bad thing, and frequently connected to the Law. In part this is because Paul says things like, no human being will be justified by "works of the law" in God's sight (Romans 3:20) and "we hold that one is justified by faith apart from works of the law" (Romans 3:28). Sounds bad, doesn't it?

But justification by faith has always been true at all times throughout history. No one ever earned salvation because of merit gained by following some rules, no matter how perfectly (Romans 3:20). People have always been saved by grace through faith. Have you ever wondered why people like Able, Enoch, Noah, Abraham, Sarah, Isaac, Jacob, Joseph, Moses, Rahab, David, Samuel and so on (Hebrews 11) are held up as examples of faith to follow, when they were in the "old testament" time? How could they have been saved? The difference is they did not have "alone faith," or faith without works. They both trusted God <u>and</u> did what He said.

Faith does not invalidate the Law. Faith and Law work together with love and the Spirit to save. (Romans 3:31) Faith is trusting obedience. Misuse of the Law does not mean the Law is the problem. Some, such as Pharisees and other Nicolaitans, think that the Law is a means to earn salvation. It never was. "Faith was counted to Abraham as righteousness" (Genesis 26:5, Romans 4:9) because he believed God, and showed that belief by doing what He said. We know that Abraham believed God because he did what God told him (Genesis 26:5). As said by James, when Abraham offered up his son on the altar it was evidence of belief, and "a person is justified by works not by faith alone" (James 2:21-26). It is not "works" that is the problem, or the Law. The problem is "alone" faith. Faith includes works in keeping with repentance.

What is a "work of the Law" anyway? Giving? Taking care of widows and orphans? Free will animal barbecues? Avoiding immorality? A few holidays? A Sabbath rest? All of these are parts of the Law, and if we look close, we see that "works of the law" are good things. So why would Paul say that these works would not justify us to God? I think the writer of Hebrews says it well.

> Hebrews 4:2, AV. For unto us was the gospel preached, as well as unto them: but the word preached did not profit them, not being mixed with faith in them that heard it.

Faith is trust plus obedience. If we do not have faith, works of the Law are useless for purchasing salvation. If we say we have faith but have no works, we do not have faith either. God wants our hearts, souls, mind and strength. If in faith and love, we follow all of His commands, it will result in salvation. Doesn't God "command men everywhere to repent" (Acts 17:30)? His Word, both written and in the person of our Messiah, saves us. We show that we have faith by works of the Law, motivated by a heart of flesh, on which His Laws are written. Works of the Law are not worthless. Working without faith, love and the Spirit is worthless.

In my opinion, Paul was primarily thinking of the oral law. As I have already said, rabbis had loaded up the written law with all sorts of oral traditions, many of which were not part of the Law as Jesus demonstrated. Modern Nicolaitans do the same thing. How many times have you heard laws in the Church that are not in the Bible? The Church has laws that forbid such things as dancing, music, musical instruments, men and women swimming together, smoking, cussing, and on and on. I'm not saying these laws and others like them are bad (although many are really stupid) but I am saying that none of them are in the Bible. These "works of the law" do not save anyone. No one will be justified in God's sight sufficient for salvation by doing any of them. Paul was addressing the philosophies of men that were popping up all over the place, not God's Word. We can see that those philosophies continue to this day in the avoidance of God's Laws and the increase of men's.

Israel Only. Some Nicolaitans have to stretch incredibly far in their Greek, philosophical quest to direct people away from the Word. One of the many examples is that the Law was "for the nation, not for individuals" as Andy Stanley says. I'm not sure what he means, which I think is part of the reason Nicolaitans say such weird stuff. Maybe they want to look really smart and keep people guessing as to whether the Bible actually says what they claim. Does he mean the individual can't follow it? That doesn't make sense. Of course we can follow it (Deuteronomy 30:14;

Romans 10:8). Does he mean that it is for government only, not for individual salvation? That doesn't make sense either. Salvation has always been individual and always by grace through faith, even when the Law was given. Perhaps he means The Law was for Israel only. In that case many prophets must have misspoken, because they pronounced judgments on the nations for not doing what God said (Jeremiah 25:12-13, 15-38 and others).

Law existed before the Law was given at Sinai. In <u>Whole Bible Christianity</u>[8] I list more than 40 instances of laws, that are part of the Sinai laws, showing up in the Bible way before Mt. Sinai. God's Word has always regulated people and nations. How many times does a prophet communicate God's judgments on other nations for not following His commands? How will God judge the nations in His day of wrath during the Tribulation if His Word is not applicable to the nations? God expects everyone, covenant member or not, to obey. He will judge nations and individuals whether they like it or not.

Taking the statement in its plain meaning, it's a lie and has zero support from the Word. The Law was for the nation AND individuals. All we have to do to disprove it is read.

> Deuteronomy 32:45–47, ESV. And when Moses had finished speaking all these words to all Israel, he said to them, "Take to heart all the words by which I am warning you today, that you may command them to your children, that they may be careful to do all the words of this law. For it is no empty word for you, but your very life, and by this word you shall live long in the land that you are going over the Jordan to possess."

If we are supposed to teach the Law to our children, that hardly seems to be a "national" thing only. It is obviously an individual thing as well. It is true that one individual could mess things up for the nation. Achan did it when he held back some of

---

[8] Whole Bible Christianity, Blessings Pressed Down and Overflowing, by Bruce S. Bertram, The Word of God Ministries, 2016, page 123.

the devoted things from Jericho (Joshua 7:1), and David did it when he took a census of Israel (2 Samuel 24:1). But that doesn't mean the Law was only national. One individual can also make a difference in leading to righteousness. See the kings of Israel (Judah) for instance such as Jehoshaphat, Josiah and Hezekiah.

It is also true that Israel as a nation was supposed to live by the Covenant and create an environment which other nations would find compelling. If they did it right blessings would be pressed down and overflowing, and nations would recognize that God was the one blessing.

> Deuteronomy 4:7–8, ESV. For what great nation is there that has a god so near to it as the LORD our God is to us, whenever we call upon him? And what great nation is there, that has statutes and rules so righteous as all this law that I set before you today?

If the Covenant is "not for individuals," how in the world do we understand these verses?

> Deuteronomy 29:14–15, ESV. It is not with you alone that I am making this sworn covenant, but with whoever is standing here with us today before the LORD our God, and with whoever is not here with us today.

At the very least, this means the kids. The truth of the Word shows us that the Constitution God set up for Israel was both national and individual. We can compare this to the illustration of the Body that Paul gives us in Romans 12. Individuals do their part, following God's instructions in daily living. Groups of individuals convene to carry out corporate rules such as a thorough investigation of something wrong. The nation as a whole would thrive if individuals followed His instructions from the heart.

> Isaiah 1:27–28, ESV. Zion shall be redeemed by justice, and those in her who repent, by righteousness. But rebels and sinners shall be broken together, and those who forsake the LORD shall be consumed.

Nations don't have eternal life; repentant individuals do. Experience as well as the Bible record tells us that evil affects everyone, not just the individual. Paul says "Purge the evil person from among you" (1 Corinthians 5:13; compare to Deuteronomy 17:7, 21:21, 22:21 and others) because evil affects everyone. God was dwelling in the midst of Israel, which required them to bury their toilet leavings so God wouldn't see "anything indecent among you" (Deuteronomy 23:13). I'm fine with that because I wouldn't want to step in it either! Imagine how much indecency is among us now because we refuse to follow His commands!

This is really the point of the Bible. It's not just following some rules. It is a life of loving God as He loves us. All people are to cling to every word from God as if it is life, love and fruit of the Spirit. Enoch did it. Noah did it. Abraham did it. Moses, Joshua, Esther, Ruth, Boaz and David did it. Some of the kings of Israel did it. The prophets did it. Jesus did it. The apostles did it. The first century congregations did it, making them a wonderful example to follow. Which begs the question, "Why don't modern Churches follow their example?"

7 Good Shepherds

Jeremiah 23:21–22, ESV. "I did not send the prophets, yet they ran; I did not speak to them, yet they prophesied. But if they had stood in my council, then they would have proclaimed my words to my people, and they would have turned them from their evil way, and from the evil of their deeds.

We've done a lot of work uncovering the character and work of a bad shepherd or Nicolaitan. So now what does the Bible say about good shepherds? Well, I'm glad you asked that. There are plenty of examples and lots of Scripture that help us determine whom we should be following. God identifies for us the characteristics of a godly leader all over the place.

A good contrast to help us understand false teachers and their ways is to look at the descriptions of a true teacher. Paul tells us in 1 Timothy that the aim of a true teacher is "love that issues from a pure heart and good conscience and a sincere faith" (1 Timothy 1:5). In the same book he also lays out the qualifications of an overseer as "above reproach, husband of one wife, sober-minded, self-controlled, respectable, hospitable, able to teach, not a drunkard, not violent but gentle, not quarrelsome, not a lover of money, (managing) his own household well, with all dignity keeping his children submissive...not a recent convert or he may become puffed up with conceit...well thought of by outsiders..." (1 Timothy 3:2-7). Ezekiel 34 describes shepherds, good and bad.

Remember, Timothy was at Ephesus, one of the congregations that get a letter from Jesus in Revelation. Paul spent a great deal of time in Ephesus and in the letter to the Ephesians speaks a bunch about love. Sentiment is a part of love, but is not love all by itself. Love is laying down your life, first for God in obedience and then for our brothers and sisters. Laying down your life means to choose God's ways first then live them and share them with others. Even at the cost of position, authority and pride.

Serving. The easiest way to characterize a true teacher, as opposed to a Nicolaitan or follower of Jezebel and Balaam, is the word "servant." A true teacher is a servant of God and of believers.

Think about the job of a servant. If you had a servant, they would do whatever you told them to do. A servant of God does what God tells him or her to do. In every biblical case, a servant of God follows His instructions. The most basic instructions are those in the Law. So a servant of God first and foremost follows the Law. He or she may have additional instructions they feel came from God, but if a leader claims to be from God he or she will not only follow the Law but will not speak against it.

> John 7:17–19, ESV. If anyone's will is to do God's will, he will know whether the teaching is from God or whether I am speaking on my own authority. The one who speaks on his own authority seeks his own glory; but the one who seeks the glory of him who sent him is true, and in him there is no falsehood. Has not Moses given you the law? Yet none of you keeps the law. Why do you seek to kill me?"

A servant speaking for God seeks God's glory, not his own. He will speak the Words of God, which at the heart are those in the Law of Moses with clarifying instructions from Jesus and the apostles. We are slaves of God, in servitude to righteousness.

Speaking the Words of God gets one in a lot of trouble with the establishment. The Nicolaitan, even the Nicolaitan that is genuine but misled, will generally seek his own glory, and will speak things such as "the law was fulfilled and eliminated by Jesus" or "civil and ceremonial laws didn't get past the cross" or "the Church has replaced Israel" and other such proclamations.

> Matthew 5:19, ESV. Therefore whoever relaxes one of the least of these commandments and teaches others to do the same will be called least in the kingdom of heaven, but whoever does them and teaches them will be called great in the kingdom of heaven.

Humility. Perhaps the leading characteristic of a true leader/servant is real humility.

Matthew 18:4, ESV. Whoever humbles himself like this child is the greatest in the kingdom of heaven.

Proverbs 3:34, ESV. Toward the scorners he is scornful, but to the humble he gives favor.

But let's take a look at the meaning of the words "humility," "humble," and "meek." Pharaoh was not humble because he did not do what God said. He refused to listen to Moses, let Israel go, and let them worship Him (Exodus, specifically 10:3). Moses, on the other hand, was very meek; "more than all people who were on the face of the earth" (Numbers 12:3). The words for humble, humility or meek generally are defined as "bowing down" or "bowed." A humble or meek person bows himself before God, acknowledges God, and worships by obeying every word God speaks. He recognizes the Messiah Jesus, and submits to all of His words too, because the words of Jesus are the same as the words of the Father. In fact, a humble person takes the Words of the Bible as the Words of God. It doesn't matter if God speaks the words directly, or if He certifies them as a witness of other people's words and actions.

Humility or meekness is associated with poor, meaning not wealthy. I don't think this would mean totally lacking in the ability to feed or house a family, but I do think it means not very wealthy compared to people who are wealthy and proud (not godly). Wealth has a tendency to make a person forget God. God blesses with health or money or other good things, and sadly, Nicolaitans do not acknowledge the source of the blessings. Wealth is not a guarantee that godliness is missing because God desires to bless His children with goodness. Abraham, Job and David were wealthy. Conversely, lack of wealth is not a guarantee of godliness either. You don't have to be poor to be a believer; it's just that wealth complicates a lot of things. We have examples of wealthy humble men or women, and we have examples of poor who are prideful. Maybe the best way to phrase it is that the presence or absence of wealth does not affect a true teacher from God. He or she follows God in all things.

Meek does not mean pushover, either. A meek or humble teacher exhibits what we might call a "non-confrontational" character when delivering the words of God, but can certainly get confrontational if defending those same words (or believers) from false teachers or unbelievers. Abraham took 318 people from his household to challenge the four kings and rescue his nephew Lot (Genesis 14:8-16). David dodged Saul and refused to kill him when he had several chances, but was a mighty king in battle against those that attacked Israel. Moses led Israel in battle against Sihon and Og, prayed for judgment against Korah so that the earth swallowed him up, and yet didn't fight back and relied on God to defend him when Israel grumbled. Jesus humbled himself by following everything the Father wanted Him to do, even to death on a cross, yet chased people out of the temple with whips and will be coming back with armies and judgment. No, meekness does not mean someone who will not stand up for the faith. It means someone who is gentle yet firm in faith, and delivers God's Words without hammering on people, but at the same time can destroy calf idols or hate the works of the Nicolaitans.

Abraham. In the case of Abraham, we have an example of a man who listened to God, even to almost sacrificing the son promised to him and connected to the blessing of many nations. He went after the four kings who captured his nephew Lot with only 318 people, but also interceded for the righteous of Sodom and Gomorrah with Jesus. The reason he received the promise was "because Abraham obeyed my voice and kept my charge, my commandments, my statutes, and my laws" (Genesis 26:5). Abraham wasn't afraid to take up arms if needed and he followed God in humility and meekness.

Moses. Almost killed as a baby and rescued by the daughter of Pharaoh, Moses probably received the best schooling Egypt had to offer. Later he was a shepherd for forty years in the wilderness of Midian. When God talked with him at the burning bush, Moses was eighty years old and he was 120 years old when he died. In our biblical record we have the direct statement that "the man Moses was very meek, more than all people who were on the face of the earth" (Numbers 12:3). He didn't make a living off of his ministry; "I have not taken one donkey from them, and I have not harmed one of them" (Numbers 16:15) and exhibited anger when it was needed (same verse) for Korah's rebellion. He faithfully delivered all God's Words even when confronted by a hostile audience. Moses messed up once by striking the rock instead of speaking to it, and paid for it. Still, in his meekness he was an effective leader and witness for God.

David. A man after God's own heart according to 1 Samuel 13:14, David started out as a shepherd, lived on the run from Saul for seven years, and became the most famous king of Israel. He followed the Law (Psalm 18:20-24), he wouldn't kill Saul when he had a couple chances, and he repented for sin immediately. A musician also, he wrote a large portion of the Psalms which show how much he depended on God and worked hard to follow Him. David was given the promises of Abraham (1 Samuel 7:11-16) and was told by God that while he couldn't build the Temple, from him would come a king to sit on the throne forever. He screwed up too in the episode with Uriah and his wife for which he lost a son. Even the best of our examples did wrong on occasion, except One.

Yeshua/Jesus. Speaking of the leadership example who did not sin, Jesus was born into humble circumstances as the human baby of a carpenter. He received what was probably a standard education (He could read and write) and was extremely well-versed in the Scriptures or Tanakh. He was able to ask insightful questions of the rabbis when as young as the age of 12 (Luke 2:41-49) but not much else is known about His childhood as a son of

David. He started His public preaching with the message of repentance (Mark 1:14-15) and taught only what the Father wanted (John 5:19, 30, 46-47, 14:10, 17:8). He was a servant of the Father in every way "and being found in human form, he humbled himself by becoming obedient to the point of death, even death on a cross" (Philippians 2:8). His will was the Father's will and His Words are the Father's Words. He is the ultimate example of a true teacher or shepherd (Ezekiel 34:15-24), meek and humble, but was also zealous for His Father's house (John 2:17). Yeshua is the example for all believers to follow, and leaders most of all. He followed all of God's Words in every instance without question or doubt and told us we are to be perfect as our heavenly Father is perfect.

> Matthew 5:46–48, ESV. For if you love those who love you, what reward do you have? Do not even the tax collectors do the same? And if you greet only your brothers, what more are you doing than others? Do not even the Gentiles do the same? You therefore must be perfect, as your heavenly Father is perfect.

Peter. This example of a true teacher was one of the first called to the side of Jesus. He was a fisherman by trade, and probably didn't have much of an advanced education. He watched and learned for a long time, made the first confession of Jesus as the Messiah (Matthew 16:16) and in the book of Acts is shown to be a bold and knowledgeable preacher of the gospel. Pete was kind of up and down as he tried to figure out a balance between his Jewish upbringing and fellowshipping with Gentiles. Paul had to correct him when he withdrew from eating with the Gentiles in Galatia (Galatians 2:14) because of some Jewish visitors. But he did learn a balance (Acts 10:34-35) and wrote two letters to Jewish believers living over a wide geographic area. He was one of the three on the mount of Transfiguration but he was also the one to deny Jesus three times. Peter was a little grieved when Jesus asked him three times if he loved Jesus and to "feed my sheep" (John

21:15-17). His ministry was mostly to Jewish people, while Paul's was mostly to Gentiles. He faltered some following Jesus in the beginning, but stabilized later and is a pillar in the body of Christ.

Paul. Another former Nicolaitan like Nicodemus, Paul was zealous for the Lord, or what He thought was for the Lord. According to his own testimony (Philippians 3:3-6), he was a Hebrew of Hebrews and a Pharisee. He called himself "the circumcision" but "put no confidence in the flesh." He was so zealous as a Pharisee that he persecuted believers in Jesus and stood by while Stephen was stoned to death. As educated as he was, Jesus thought he needed further instruction and initiated a graduate course to further his understanding of God. He was a quick learner, "advancing in Judaism beyond many of my own age" (Galatians 1:14) so this stood him in good stead during his graduate studies (17 years according to Galatians 1:18 and 2:1). When he realized that Jesus was in fact the promised Messiah, he became just as zealous in preaching the good news of God with us. Unlike the Nicolaitan teaching that he converted to Christianity and ditched the Law, he did not stop following the Law.

Paul observed feasts (20:6,16, 24:17, 18) fasts (27:9) vows (18:18; 21:23-26) Sabbath (13:14, 42, 44, 16:13, 17:2, 18:4) circumcision (16:3) temple worship (22:17, 24:11, 17, 18) teaching from the Law and the Prophets (28:23) and keeping the Law (21:24, 22:3, 23:6, 24:14). Paul was obviously a model of a law-following Jew before and after meeting Jesus. He did not ditch the Law, did not regard it as "old," and traveled much of the earth telling people about the Law along with the traditions (1 Corinthians 11:2). These traditions were from the OT, because he tells the Colossians to beware of human tradition (Colossians 2:8).

He was humble in his graduate seminary course with Jesus, changing immediately from persecuting believers to being one. He saw the truth and embraced it. He was baptized (probably a second time at least) and went right to the synagogues "saying, He is the son of God" (Acts 9:20). How many present-day Nicolaitans would switch this quick if shown they were wrong by the Word?

John. When I think of John I see a curious mix of passion (he was a "son of thunder" with James his brother Mark 3:17), intensity and love. He was probably the apostle who "Jesus loved" (John 13:23) was present at the Transfiguration with Peter and his brother James (Matthew 17) and wrote the gospel of John, the three letters of 1, 2, and 3 John, and the book of Revelation. It seems he was the longest lived of the apostles, lasting until almost 100 years old (assuming he was about 30, around the same age as Jesus when he started his public ministry). In his writings, he speaks probably the most about love, abiding, obedience and God's commandments.

1 John 5:3, ESV. For this is the love of God, that we keep his commandments. And his commandments are not burdensome.

All of these true teacher examples followed God's Law. They were humble, not always poor, but meek because they changed immediately when shown they were wrong. All except One did things wrong but repented quickly and persevered in following God. They are the definition of faithfulness to God's ways and Word. All of them glorified God with their teaching, not themselves. Loving God stands out all over their lives and teachings within a framework of the Law. The Law was never a problem for any of them because doing what God says was a way of life. They taught and lived the fullness of everything God told them to do. Truly, they are shepherds we can copy.

Luke 17:10, ESV. So you also, when you have done all that you were commanded, say, 'We are unworthy servants; we have only done what was our duty.' "

8 Repent

Psalm 119:92–93, ESV. If your law had not been my delight, I would have perished in my affliction. I will never forget your precepts, for by them you have given me life.

Bringing my definitions of a Nicolaitan together, we get a complete picture of most teachers in the modern Church. Starting with the brief mentions in Revelation 2, their teachings are hated by Jesus. Works that are hated by Jesus include haughty eyes (pride), lying words, hypocrisy, and falsely speaking the words of Jesus. The meaning of the word Nicolaitan is "destruction" or "victory over" lay people, which points to a domineering attitude similar to Pharisees. They are associated with feathered friends along the lines of Jezebel and Balaam who use sexual immorality and idolatry to pry believers apart from their Messiah. They are probably Gentile versions of hypocrites such as Pharisees and Sadducees, and are opposite of the Good Shepherd Yeshua.

Rephrasing a little, Church/synagogue Nicolaitans obtain power over others using education, wealth or other worldly success. They misuse the power they gain like bad shepherds, feeding false teachings to the flock that they claim are from God's Word, but are not found in the Bible. Like Pharisees, their outside-the-Bible rulings and traditions weigh believers down with a yoke too heavy for most to bear and deny the One Body. Modern Nicolaitans are pastors, priests, popes, ministers, rabbis, elders, board members, Sunday school teachers, home Bible study leaders, self-identified prophets and Stake presidents (Mormon leaders).

Ezekiel 34:3–6 ESV. You eat the fat, you clothe yourselves with the wool, you slaughter the fat ones, but you do not feed the sheep. The weak you have not strengthened, the sick you have not healed, the injured you have not bound up, the strayed you have not brought back, the lost you have not sought, and with force and harshness you have ruled them. So they were scattered, because there was no shepherd, and they became food for all the wild beasts. My sheep were scattered;

they wandered over all the mountains and on every high hill.
My sheep were scattered over all the face of the earth, with
none to search or seek for them.

Church Nicolaitan tactics include rebuilding the dogma
wall dividing people, manipulating emotions, clinging to Church
tradition, protecting the Church tower at all costs, power grabs,
speaking falsely for Jesus, using plausible arguments in place of
the Word, dodging biblical questions, disconnecting parts of the
Bible from other parts, controlling salvation, hate for Israel and
wrongly dividing the Word. Not all Nicolaitans use all of these
tactics because there are different styles and combinations. So one
Nicolaitan might not hate Israel but use most of the other tactics.

Then there are the philosophies of men which add to the
mix. These philosophies might look good but have little or no
backup from the Bible. Blind faith in dogma is common in their
followers. Foundations built by them are sandy because they only
contain a few verses, or just focus on Paul and the gospels. They
are full of BS, subtly blaming God's Law as being inadequate for
living. Immaturity is a hallmark of both the shepherds and the
people learning from them, as they just go over and over the
elementary principles of Hebrews 6:1-3. Idol worship is evident in
a Jesus bled dry of the living oracles, leaving a hollow husk of a
permissive nice guy. They appropriate the funeral parlor makeup
of Greek culture for their Jesus idol, so He doesn't look so dead,
and it works as long as they "think" or "feel" they are following
Him. Alone faith, unattached from works in keeping with
repentance, is a favorite theme, as well as a slew of other ignorant
ideas such as a Law that is slavery, death or nailed to the cross.

You might have been speculating while reading through
some spots in this book about the reasons for writing. Perhaps I
seem a bit over the top or really aggravated. Maybe you think I'm
being too mean, or too general. I could have an ax to grind, taking

personal pot shots at Church figures because I've been hurt in some way. Well, I have to say, you would be right.

I do have an ax to grind. I *was* hurt many times in the Church, robbed of maturity, fruit of the Spirit, touching God and abundant life. I *am* taking shots at Church leaders that act like Nicolaitans. I don't hate the people, but like Jesus, I hate their works. It upsets me that so many seemingly good teachers are keeping churchgoers divided, and their flocks blocked off, from the many wonderful benefits of the whole of God's Word.

But my motivation is not just from those things. I am coming from what I believe is the same frame of reference as my Messiah. He has an ax to grind with all those who abolish the meaning of His Word, and who block entry into His kingdom, while they refuse to go in themselves. Nicolaitans personally hurt Him when He was falsely accused, beaten and nailed to a cross, and He is hurt still more when bad shepherds rob His sheep of the abundant life in His Word. Jesus takes pot shots, if you can call the seven letters of Revelation or the descriptions in Matthew 23 pot shots, at all those who claim they speak for Him when in fact they speak for their master the deceiver. He hates the works of the Nicolaitans and approves of believers who hate them also.

You'd be tweezed also if you had been denied the wonderful blessings of a whole Bible walk. It's not just me that is affected either. It's you and many others yearning for life abundant, hungering and thirsting for righteousness and for touching God. Nicolaitans are denying these blessings to all believers.

I will probably get criticized for painting with a brush that is too broad. I'll be told I have seemingly taken a couple of tiny mentions of people we know very little about and convicted a huge number of really nice guys in the Church. In my advance defense, I will say first that Jesus did it with the Pharisees. They as a group were so removed from the Word, and so corrupt, that the few like Nicodemus were not enough to save them from their just condemnation. Second, the bulk of my proofs for modern

Nicolaitanism are the deceptive, philosophical teachings of men, and the immorality, that places most of the Church squarely in the camp of the teachings that Jesus hates. It's not hard to figure out.

Leaven. Speaking of tiny mentions, remember I said that Jesus warns us to beware of the leaven of the Pharisees (Luke 12:1), which is hypocrisy. In a manner similar to Pharisee teaching, the hated Nicolaitan works started out perhaps small, like a tiny bit of leaven. But Nicolaitan teachings with hypocrisy have worked their way through churches a little at a time until the whole Church is corrupt like Sardis. The modern Pharisees or Nicolaitans have had centuries to refine their teachings and work them throughout the Church (and synagogue, temple or whatever). They set up extra-biblical "orthodox" teachings, then point fingers at those who would rather follow the Bible. Like the wizard in that famous movie, they are desperate to keep you from looking behind the curtain. Hypocrites! Serpents! Brood of vipers! Blind guides! Lawless! Thus Jesus warned His children about false shepherds such as Pharisees, Sadducees, Balaam, Jezebel and Nicolaitans.

> Matthew 23:27–28, ESV. "Woe to you, scribes and Pharisees, hypocrites! For you are like whitewashed tombs, which outwardly appear beautiful, but within are full of dead people's bones and all uncleanness. So you also outwardly appear righteous to others, but within you are full of hypocrisy and lawlessness.

There are good people in the Churches; non-Nicolaitans who exhibit some of the best of character traits taught by Jesus. The story of George Müller (1805-1898) and his orphanages bring tears to my eyes when I hear it. Most universities in the United States were started to train ministers. The push for public education initially came from the Church because it was desired for people to learn to read their Bibles (an original reason for Sunday schools too).

There are all kinds of good deeds done on the down low that most never hear about. I would say that these bright spots, however, show up in spite of the Nicolaitans and only slightly because of them. It is due to God's Word, though hit and miss or even full of holes. The bright spots have hearts of flesh rather than stone, accepting the seed of the Word and bearing fruit thirty, sixty or a hundred fold. A bad tree cannot bear good fruit (Matthew 7:17-18, 12:33; Luke 6:43). It is sad testimony to the false teachings that those churchgoers who should, as a group, show the wonderful fruit of the Holy Spirit, do not. Instead, they show fruit such as hypocrisy, immorality, ignorance of the Bible and close-mindedness in refusing to repent and learn.

There were also bright spots Jesus highlighted about the seven congregations of Revelation. Well, six of them anyway. Then again, of some, He also said, "But I have this against you." Ephesus toiled and had patient endurance, testing false apostles. "But I have this against you, that you have abandoned the love you had at first." Smyrna had tribulations and poverty, and were slandered by Jews who were not Jews, but would need to "be faithful unto death." Pergamum had Satan's throne yet held fast to the name of Jesus and didn't deny His faith. "But I have a few things against you" in that you have some who hold the teaching of Balaam and Nicolaitans.

Thyatira had works, love, faith, service and patient endurance and latter works that exceeded the first. But they also had Jezebel and her followers. Sardis had the reputation of being alive but was dead, though they had a few names that had not soiled their garments. Philadelphia had good works and patient endurance, and they were the only congregation Jesus didn't criticize. Laodicea was a lukewarm lost cause who thought they needed nothing, but Jesus said they were wretched, pitiable, poor, blind and naked. Their only hope was to use their wealth to buy from Jesus gold, eye salve and white garments (works in keeping with repentance). We, also, need to heed the message of Jesus when He tells the modern Church "I have this against you." We may think we need nothing, but Jesus has a different opinion.

Six of the congregations in Revelation were barely hanging on by their fingernails. Philadelphia was also barely hanging on, but Jesus was strengthening them. If we take these congregations to also be examples of groups who wear His name today, or groups within Churches, as I think we can, then the message from Jesus to them, or us, is REPENT. The modern Church and the Nicolaitans would do well to learn from these congregations.

Many Nicolaitan teachers look at the seven letters and cannot identify the bad guys (except maybe the Jews) or the hated teachings other than an historical application. They can't figure it out because they look everywhere but the mirror. Jesus was telling those congregations to repent, and He is telling all modern congregations the same thing. He sees some good things. Some of us are toiling with patient endurance and testing false apostles like the Ephesians did. Some are poor, suffering and dying like Smyrna, but will gain a crown of life. There are those whose works show love and faith and patient endurance like Thyatira. The congregations like Pergamum are enduring Satan's attacks but still are not denying His faith. Some Churches, as in Sardis, have a few names worthy to walk in white. Others, such as Laodicea, are toast.

Among all the good things in the congregations, there is lots of bad. Like Sardis, we have the reputation of being alive but we are dead. As in Ephesus, we have lost our first love. Neither cold nor hot and merely lukewarm, too many are tolerating the teachings of Jezebel, Balaam, and the Nicolaitans. Some say, "I am rich, I have prospered, and I need nothing" when in reality they are wretched, pitiable, poor, blind and naked. We need to wake up, buy from Jesus gold refined by fire, white garments (works not hated by Him) and salve for our eyes (Jesus in all His Words). We need to clothe ourselves so the shame of our nakedness will not be seen and use the salve to heal our eyes so we can see. Those He loves He reproves and disciplines, "so be zealous and repent."

A Church sign I saw recently at a local Church called Redlands Community said, "Teach me your way, oh Lord." This is a phrase from several Psalms (25:4, 27:11, 86:11, 119:26 for starters) and every one points to "your way" as the Law. The Law is "His ways," it is what Jesus delivered and lived, and what He commands us to obey. It is massive hypocrisy to advertise "teach me your way" when there is no intention of following His Way at all. In fact, Joe Gross, the pastor of this Church, rescinded an invitation to attend made by one of their members to our family because, as he said after viewing our website, we were "all about rules and regulations!" In his view, the living oracles are bad.

Can a Nicolaitan repent? Yes, they can. Repentance is always an option while anyone is alive. Everyone needs to repent on occasion anyway. Even Daniel repented (Daniel 9). The question is *will* the Nicolaitan repent? That is tougher to answer. It depends on the heart. Are they really believers? Are they hungering and thirsting after God's Word? Are they like Nicodemus who sought a one-on-one schooling session with Jesus? Will they risk their careers or income? Many of them have position and power they might have to give up if they follow the whole of God's Word. Churches are intolerant of those who depart from Church dogma. Peer pressure is hard to fight, and the humiliation of a loss of income or position makes it even harder. The other Nicolaitans don't like to let go of a fellow son of hell.

These people claim to speak for God, and tell us authoritatively that certain things are true, when they are just out and out lying. They are lying in order to get us in a club where they can milk us for "tithes" and build monuments to their egos, instead of teaching us to walk according to all of God's living oracles. You can't imagine (but you will see it for yourself one day hopefully) the infusion of the fruit of the Spirit and abundant life when you discover that all of the Word is for you, too.

For years when I was in the Nicolaitan camp I denied myself the beauty, the life, and the love that was in every Word

God speaks, including what some call the Law. I barely knew God because I barely knew and hardly practiced His Words. I tried and tried to connect with God in the approved Church ways, and I could see and touch Him sometimes. But I faded in and out, in immaturity, because Nicolaitans blocked the practice of His whole Word. I thank Him that the salve I purchased worked, the log is gone, and I can see to take in all of His Words and do them.

Twenty years ago, I was an elder at Valley Bible Church here locally. As I started to learn that there were more blessings to a walk with Jesus than I had previously known, I was told to stop teaching the adult Sunday school, which had gotten excellent reviews from visiting pastors. Then I had to stop teaching from the pulpit. Next, some accused me of exerting pressure on the congregation to do the same things my family was doing.

Because I was an elder, some of the churchgoers felt pressure to do what we were doing. We certainly didn't (and don't) want people to follow all of the Word as if it is "tradition learned by rote" (Isaiah 29:13) so I ended up resigning. It wasn't enough. The people there didn't want reminding that their lives were lacking so much of the life in the Word. We were called "dangerous" and couldn't stay, because I didn't just shut up and sit there while so many cries for the touch of God went unanswered. Since I turned my back on the stale bread and brackish water offered by "Church" I haven't looked back. I've found abundant life living on His Word alone. You can too.

A Nicolaitan is like a child that has stopped growing. It is an unnatural situation. It is not God's plan to keep us in the salvation moment and preach a Jesus idol who went back on His own Law, and whose grace is permission to sin. If we are part of God's family, the one body of Jesus, a child in God's household, slaves to righteousness, then growing and maturing and showing the fruit of the Spirit is the natural situation. If we don't grow, there is something wrong somewhere. It seems evident it is due to poor nutrition coming from a starvation diet.

The teachings of the Nicolaitans make disciples that have arrested development just like themselves. The student becomes just like the master. Instead of maturity, there is perpetual childishness, petty gossip, backbiting, anxiety, depression and other signs of high school immaturity. Instead of the fruit of the Spirit, there is a whole lot of works of the flesh. Instead of life more abundant, we have suicide, divorce, adultery and other teachings of Jezebel and Balaam, as common inside the Church as they are outside. So many are frozen in the "salvation moment" and either cannot (because of the teaching) or will not move on to the fullness of the Christ that one despairs of any change.

Naming Names. I named a few names in this book and maybe that's not fair. There are a lot of Nicolaitans that are laboring away incognito and are not as recognizable. But the famous guys are big targets and excellent examples of Nicolaitan philosophy. They help us out by setting themselves up as obvious bad examples. Sadly, there are so many such bad examples that I could fill a number of volumes with their works. I just don't have the space or the time to include all of the actors, bloggers, politicians, musicians, doctors, or authors. Some "honorable" mentions are Joel Osteen, Jimmy Swaggart, Pete Buttigieg, Rob Bell, Scott Gunn, William P. Young (The Shack), the Bakers, John McArthur, James Dobson, Greg Laurie, Mark Driscoll, Rick Warren, Jeannie Cunnion, and editors at Relevant magazine.

You might be horrified at my mention of some of the names. "John McArthur! How can you say he's a Nicolaitan! He's such a good teacher." And I would agree. He, and many like him, teaches some good things. That's the point of using him as an example. Nicolaitans *have* to teach some of the truth in order to get acceptance for the lies. A Pied Piper needs a pleasing tune to get the kids to follow.

Maybe I should be afraid of naming names, especially of respected, powerful people having huge Churches, expansive public ministries and lots of money to sue. But I'm not afraid of the powerful; I'm afraid of God. And I'm afraid for the people that the powerful lords of the flock are keeping away from maturity, fruit of the Spirit and abundant life. I have identified the works of the Nicolaitans and shown where they are wrong; they should feel free to challenge my teachings too. Give me Bible teaching unobscured by Church dogma. Instead of slicing and dicing the Word for your convenience, teach me the continuity of one faith delivered once for all to the saints. Show me your humility and servant attitude and give a defense for what you believe. Let me see your churches full of those like David, Rahab, Peter and John, instead of those full of people like Balaam, Jezebel, the Pharisees and Judas. Where are the Churches like those of Acts chapter 2?

Some Nicolaitans are kind, caring people who give their lives for what they believe. They fight the good fight, are servants, and humbly follow what they know of the Bible. When challenged, they sincerely review their position and repent if they need to change direction. Maybe some of those named and unnamed are like that and will hear what Jesus says and repent. We can only hope. I am not discounting their good works and teachings, and I'm sure that Jesus has taken note. Some are right on the border of repentance, and some try to teach the whole of God's Word as best they can in their situation. I am a nice guy too, and I care for the lost. It's just that my solution for everyone includes taking in all of His Words and doing them. Other nice guys decide that being stuck in the salvation moment is enough.

> Jeremiah 5:30–31, ESV. An appalling and horrible thing has happened in the land: the prophets prophesy falsely, and the priests rule at their direction; my people love to have it so, but what will you do when the end comes?

The End. I don't think the Church as a whole will repent. It is my opinion that all of the bureaucracies will cooperate with the beast (Revelation 18). They won't recognize him because they don't know the Word. The Catholic part of the Church will lead, but every other organization claiming to be the Church or follow God will follow. Churchgoers are unprepared for what is coming, because they follow the pastor rather than the Word. In place of strength from a mature understanding and practice of God's ways, we have a bunch of wimpy, politically correct, malnourished snowflakes mostly unwilling to consume the meat of the Word.

If an angel showed up to your town and told you to get out, would you listen? Or would you mock him and refuse to leave the danger zone because you cannot recognize the moving of the Holy Spirit? Many don't hear God because they are deaf to His Word. The average Churchgoer will not be able to hear God if He directs them to move out of the way. Churchgoers are waiting to be whisked away in a rapture, or for the Church to conquer. They are not ready for the terrible things coming on the Day of the Lord.

Jesus is calling His people to "come out of her lest you take part in her sins, lest you share in her plagues" (Revelation 18:4). So there is hope. Those who are simply misguided, and have been missing out on the nutrition of the whole Word, can partake of His bread anytime and return to the path of healthy growth. Even famous Nicolaitans can repent. God's Word has the answers for lack of maturity, stunted fruit and limited life. "He upholds the universe by the word of his power" (Hebrews 1:3). He can make the changes. If we want them. Can you hear Him calling? Shalom.

Psalm 111:7–8, ESV. The works of his hands are faithful and just; all his precepts are trustworthy; they are established forever and ever, to be performed with faithfulness and uprightness.

Appendix: Conversation with a Nicolaitan

Leviticus 19:17, ESV. "You shall not hate your brother in your heart, but you shall reason frankly with your neighbor, lest you incur sin because of him.

I had the following email exchange in September of 2018 with Roger Anghis, who was a Pastor for 12 years at Prevailing Word Ministries in Englewood, Colorado. If you try to look up Prevailing Word you'll find that there's one in Brooklyn, one in Virginia and at least one other in Texas as of this writing but there is no longer a Church of that name in Colorado. An old website address, pwmin.org, now redirects to a different website.

The article Roger wrote to which I'm referring, <u>Children Suffer Under a Silent Church</u>, Part 1 on the website News With Views, is typical of many, many such presentations all over the web as well as in everyday sermons from pastors, ministers, priests and rabbis. It had some good sentiment concerning the abuse of children and the silence of the Church. I usually don't comment or email to the author of stuff like this because there are so many and I just don't have the time. Many are also unwilling to entertain God's solutions. I responded to this one because I thought there was a chance that this guy might listen. I was wrong. Instead, he turns out to be a wonderful example of Nicolaitan teaching. He uses emotionalism and is convinced of his own rightness, but has huge gaps between what the Bible says and what he teaches. He has no answers for biblical questions. This exchange is par for the course when trying to communicate with Nicolaitans.

It starts out pretty tame, and at first the guy seems reasonable. It doesn't take long, however, for pointed questions from me about the Bible to go unanswered. He substitutes the robotic repeating of Church mantras and circular reasoning. This is not the bread of life, and it shows why people are leaving the Church and yet still continuing to follow God. The Nicolaitans have mostly taken over, and like wolves in sheep's clothing, they look and sound as if they are teaching God's Word. On closer examination, they aren't even in the ballpark. As you read, pay close attention to my use of Scripture and his refusal to directly address any of the issues I raise.

Subject: Comments on your article Children Suffer Under a Silent Church, Part 1
From: Bruce Bertram <
Date: Mon, September 03, 2018 9:46 am
To: Roger Anghis

Hello
I read your article Children Suffer Under a Silent Church, Part 1 on the website News With Views. I thought it was good, as far as it goes. However, I think you are addressing symptoms instead of causes. The cause is departure from the whole of God's Word. The Church cherry-picks the Bible text, grabbing parts it likes and discarding or assigning the other parts to the Jews. The Church thinks of itself as a separate entity, which is biblically incorrect. According to Paul, there is only one body and one faith. But the Church has created itself as a non-biblical replacement and chops up the Word to support its false teachings. There is no Church in the Bible. So the foundation and the teachings are wrong in the first place.

You speak of a Covenant, yet the Church does not function within the New Covenant. The New Covenant is a heart of flesh written with the Law by the Spirit in love. The Church has styled its practice in opposition to much of the Law, saying they follow "moral" laws but not "civil" or "ceremonial" though there are no such designations in the Scriptures. So if we teach cherry-picking, what's to keep homosexuals and other immoral people from refining the cherry-picking for themselves?

The Church sits in judgment on the Word, and then is surprised when others do it too?
Shalom, Bruce Bertram

On 9/3/2018 10:28 AM, Roger wrote:

Bruce, Thank you for your comments. I believe that it is common knowledge that the Church has departed from the full Word of God. In today's Church you have to be politically correct and that means don't say anything to upset either side of the isle. Most 'organized' Churches, Baptist, Lutheran, Methodist and so on, fall into that category and they are the reason we have, as a nation, traveled down the road we are on.

There are Churches that have refused to do that and they are predominately non-denominational. The Church I pastored for 12 years did not practice political correctness. I have always believed that if you were PC then you were probably wrong. History has proved me right. I know of many Churches that have not deviated from the true gospel and they are thriving.

Roger

As I said, he starts out okay, and it seems that we might be in agreement. But there are two problems. One is he says the "Church has departed from the full Word of God," and the second is he equates this to the "true gospel." So I asked what he meant by the "true gospel." This is always a good technique when in conversation with others, and especially Nicolaitans. Make them define their terms. Nicolaitans in particular are adept at using good-sounding words and even words from the Bible. But they define the words differently than the Bible does. Gospel is one of those words. The word literally means "good news," and the Bible defines the good news as "God with us." Hebrews 4:2 tells us that the gospel was preached to Israel at Mt. Sinai - meaning the Law. So how was the Law the "good news?" That is because God was coming to live with Israel or that "God is with us." The Law is intimately connected to the "true gospel," but notice how Roger misses the Bible message entirely.

He says some churches are thriving, but what does that really mean? Does it mean they have a lot of people? Does it mean the people know the dogma really well? Or does it mean that the people know the whole Word and live it as it was intended to be lived on a daily basis? There's a big difference. Way too many times people think the health of a Church is in its attendance numbers.

Roger also thinks that somehow non-denominational is superior to denominational. There might be a couple of superficial differences. A non-denominational Church has a different government, usually one guy in charge. Denominations are controlled by a central bureaucracy and usually own the properties. But one is not superior to the other when it comes to Nicolaitans and false teaching. They are all prone to pride, immaturity and lack of abundant life. It's just a style difference. No matter the flavor or appearance, Nicolaitans are still on the wrong track and producing bad fruit, some of which you'll see in the following exchanges.

Subject: Re: Comments on your article Children Suffer Under a Silent Church, Part 1
From: Bruce Bertram
Date: Mon, September 03, 2018 10:52 am
To: Roger

Hi Roger
Thanks for the reply. Question: What is the "true gospel?"
Bruce

On 9/3/2018 11:07 AM, Roger wrote:

Every Word from Jesus Christ.

Subject: Re: Comments on your article Children Suffer Under a Silent Church, Part 1
From: Bruce Bertram
Date: Mon, September 03, 2018 11:47 am
To: Roger

So that would mean the Mosaic (as some call it) Law, wouldn't it? All of it?

114

On 9/3/2018 12:07 PM, Roger wrote:

Only part. Jesus came to fulfill the law. Part of the Mosaic laws was animal sacrifice. That is no longer needed as Jesus was the final sacrifice, Heb_7:27 Who needeth not daily, as those high priests, to offer up sacrifice, first for his own sins, and then for the people's: for this he did once, when he offered up himself. Heb_10:12 But this man, after he had offered one sacrifice for sins for ever, sat down on the right hand of God; Yet tithing remains as an act of obedience and faith.

If the gospel is "all the words of Jesus," and Jesus and God are one, then the Law given at Sinai would be included in all the words of Jesus and therefore the gospel. But notice how "all of the words of Jesus" becomes "part of the words of Jesus" without missing a beat. He doesn't even notice his inconsistency and logical fallacies.

Lots of Nicolaitans also love to go the animal sacrifice portion of the Law and use the philosophy of men that the Christ was the final sacrifice. They ignore the biblical fact that animal sacrifices never saved anyone in the first place. They were memorials of the sacrifice of the Christ (yes, you can have a memorial before something happens). They also ignore the fact that Ezekiel describes a future temple (Ezekiel 40-47) where animal sacrifices resume, which seems to be used by Jesus in the Millennial Kingdom. How can this be, according to the arguments the Church makes about sacrifices? How could Jesus make or accept sacrifices in the millennium if He eliminated sacrifices because they don't save anyone? No wonder Christian college freshmen are such easy targets for college professors! They are getting tremendously inconsistent dogmatic teaching like this from Nicolaitan leaders instead of solid Bible teaching.

Watch now as Roger starts to get deeper into confusion and double-talk.

Subject: Re: Comments on your article Children Suffer Under a Silent Church, Part 1

From: Bruce Bertram
Date: Mon, September 03, 2018 3:47 pm
To: Roger

Um, your contention that Jesus came to fulfill (meaning eliminate some or all) is not supported by Scripture. Fulfill means to "fill up full." Same word as is used in Colossians 2:9 ("For in him dwelleth all the fulness of the Godhead bodily").

The sacrifices never did save anyone. They were only effective because they were memorials or reminders of the crucifixion ("the lamb slain from the foundation of the world" Revelation 13:10). There will be a Temple in the millennial kingdom (Ezekiel 40-47) where sacrifices will be offered.

If Jesus eliminated the sacrifices, then He eliminated the tithe also, because it was primarily for the priests, widows and orphans. And if it "remains as an act of obedience and faith" then so does the rest of the Law. For the same reasons. The same rationale used to dismiss sections of the Law is used by the immoral to justify their behavior. Either it is all applicable or none of it is. When we get Jesus we get all of His words. As I said, the New Covenant is the Law written on a heart of flesh. The "new" part is the heart, not the Word.

This is what I mean when I talk about cherry-picking and is exactly why Children Suffer Under a Silent Church.

Shalom, Bruce

On 9/3/2018 8:17 PM, Roger wrote:

Bruce, you say that His coming to fulfill the law is not supported in scripture: Mat_5:17 Think not that I am come to destroy the law, or the prophets: I am not come to destroy, but to fulfil.
The sacrifices only covered the sin. It isn't eliminate it and no, their blood didn't save anyone, never said it did.

His sacrifice did NOT eliminate the tithe. Paul spoke about receiving the offerings for the benefit of the giver: Php_4:15 Now ye Philippians know also, that in the beginning of the gospel, when I departed from Macedonia, no Church communicated with me as concerning giving and receiving, but ye only.

You have to understand that if it is still talked about AFTER the cross, as tithing is, it is still in effect. No sacrifice is mentioned after the cross, it even specifies that no further animal sacrifice is needed.

You claim of all or nothing concerning the law is a typical false teaching within the organized Church. It is even used for healing declaring that healing stopped with the last disciple. The stupidity of that is we are all disciples so healing will still occur for the faithful.

Yes, most denominations 'cherry pick' scripture and it is wrong to do so, but one must understand that Jesus fulfilled the law, established a new and better covenant: Heb_8:6 But now hath he obtained a more excellent ministry, by how much also he is the mediator of a better covenant, which was established upon better promises.

Yet even with a new covenant some things came through the cross and tithing is one of them. Saying all or none is a fallacy and even lacks common sense. BTW, what is written i=on the heart is the Word.

Roger

In the first paragraph of the reply Roger deliberately misquotes me. "Fulfill" is not "terminate" as I said before. It means to "confirm" or establish." The Bible does not support the "terminate" version. This goes right along with Roger misinterpreting the Word in the first place. He acknowledges that cherry-picking is wrong, but then cherry-picks to make his point by ignoring Jeremiah's new covenant.

I also want you to notice how Roger makes the argument that if something "is still talked about AFTER the crucifixion, as tithing is, it is still in effect." First, that supposition itself is suspect. There is nothing in the Word that would justify the notion crucifixion changed the Law. Second, a search of the teachings after the cross concerning the tithe reveals nothing of it. The only exception is in Hebrews 7, where the writer speaks of tithes paid to Melchizedek being different from tithes collected by the Levites. The subject is certainly NOT tithes of a paycheck to a Church, pastor, priest, rabbi, or whatever. There are some sections that speak of a gospel worker receiving some benefit from the work, and there is an application of not muzzling an ox that treads out the grain. We can give to ministries if we want, but that is not the same thing as twisting the Word to justify a tithe after first twisting it to eliminate the "ceremonial" laws.

Third, the Law IS taught after the cross. Paul says the "Law is holy, and the commandment is holy and righteous and good" (Romans 7:12). It is "spiritual" according to Romans 7:14, and it is "good, if one uses it lawfully" as he says in 1 Timothy 1:8. Hundreds of times, various authors speak of commands or commandments. We're not even counting the times mentioning the word "obedience." If Roger's logic were consistent he would acknowledge this, but he studiously avoids mentioning it.

Subject: Re: Comments on your article Children Suffer Under a Silent Church, Part 1
From: Bruce Bertram
Date: Tue, September 04, 2018 11:04 am
To: Roger

As I said, eliminating the Torah is not supported by Scripture. Not even in the reference you provide. It doesn't make sense that Jesus said "I came not to destroy the law, but to destroy." Or slice-and-dice and just give us part. Obviously, on a plain reading, Jesus said, "I came not to destroy the law, but to fill it up full." You ignored my reference to Colossians 2:9 where the same word is used to describe the "fullness of the Godhead" residing in the Christ. Jesus tells us that "Scripture cannot be broken" in John 10:35. Jesus also says "until heaven and earth pass away, not an iota, not a dot, will pass from the Law until all is accomplished" and "whoever does them and teaches them will be called great in the kingdom of heaven."

As far as animal sacrifice, you said it was no longer necessary because "Jesus was the final sacrifice." With this statement you make animal sacrifice equal to the crucifixion, and by extension you were saying animal sacrifices saved. That is what I was responding to. The Tabernacle and Temple sacrifices were not equal to the crucifixion, but merely reminders. The main part of the sacrifices was to do what God said in every way, humbly submitting ourselves to our Lord. The Jews found excuses not to do what He said, sacrificing instead to their own self-image which is what idolatry really is. The Church is doing the exact same thing, changing the unchangeable Word to suit their whims. This is why children are suffering and the Church is silent. Look no further than the nearest mirror for the culprit. I say that including myself.

Sacrifices are indeed mentioned after the cross. Or they are at least implied, because the apostles centered around the Temple for a while. See Acts 2:46, 3:1, 3:3, and the real kicker Acts 5:20 where the angel says to "go and stand in the temple and speak to the people all the words of this Life." Did they also sacrifice? I'll bet you, as observant Jews, they did in fact sacrifice also. Did the Ethiopian eunuch, who had come to Jerusalem to "worship," make a sacrifice? I think it is obvious that he did. Was he a believer? I think so. A cursory examination of the book of Acts shows Paul observing feasts (20:6,16), fasts (27:9), vows (18:18; 21:23-26), Sabbath (13:14,42,44, 16:13, 17:2, 18:4), circumcision (16:3), temple worship (22:17, 24:11,17,18), teaching from the Law and the Prophets (28:23), and keeping the Law (21:24, 22:3, 23:6, 24:14). I believe you will find these actions occurring after the crucifixion.

Your Philippians 4:15 reference does not mention tithe, only giving, and that from an agreement between Paul and some of the congregations. I am not saying the tithe was eliminated because I support, defend and practice the Law as a lifestyle and discipleship method. You, on the other hand, must split and change the meaning of the Word in order to arrive at the practice you desire. Some of the Law, according to you, is gone, and some is still around. The tithe is not mentioned at all after the cross except for Hebrews 7 where it is mentioned in connection to the priests. If the "Lamb was slain from the foundation of the world" which we would expect since anything Jesus does is unbounded by time, then everything, technically, is after the crucifixion.

What I meant when I said all of the Word or none of it is not the standard Church teaching that if you are going to follow the Law for salvation (which is impossible) then you must follow all of it. That is a false teaching I agree. What I meant (plainly) is that if we have God we have all of His Word. On the other hand if we pick and choose then I am saying we don't have God. That is the real problem with the Church. They are whitewashed tombs full of dead men's bones. Like the Pharisees they re-define the plain meaning of the text to teach what they feel instead of what is true. This is why the children suffer and the Church is silent.

I agree that what is written on the heart is the Word. But whether you call it the Word, Law, commands, statutes, regulations, Torah, instruction, light, lamp, or the body and blood of the Messiah it is still the same. Jesus gave the Law at Sinai (that is, if you believe that Jesus and God are one) and in the Great Commission it is included in "teaching them to observe all that I have commanded you." Believers follow every word He says no matter how you describe it. And again, this is why children suffer and the Church is silent. We muzzled ourselves a long time ago when we decided to define ourselves as "not Jewish" then started a habit of treating ourselves different, splitting the Word and giving some of it to Jews and some to the "Church" (which is not mentioned in Scripture, by the way), splitting the one body of the Messiah, splitting God and splitting the faith.

The Church does not follow the New Covenant, does not teach or practice God's Word, and in general is an artificial construct by men which looks like it does what God says but really just worships themselves. I am a child of God and I suffer too. Not in the way you meant children are suffering. I suffer when I get the plain meaning of the Word twisted around and denied to me. I suffered when I was a child because I got all kinds of explanations that what I plainly read in the Word really didn't mean what it said. Then I was cut off from many good things in His Law, cut off from fruit of the Spirit, cut off from life more abundant.

Look, Roger, I'm not trying to hammer on you although you may end up placing me on the trash heap of "divisive people" which is the Church's term for people with whom they don't agree. I was like you, with the same view and arguments up until about 20 years ago. Then I found all of the Word, and all of the blessings, belonged to me. My life has been much more peaceful and full (speaking of fulfilled) since then. I wish for others the same benefits and blessings. The Church has so many barricades to it however that I sometimes despair of them getting it. Blind in one eye and can't see out of the other as my dad used to say. So I share these things with you hoping that you too will see the answer in the Word for the suffering of the children and the silence of the Church.

Shalom, Bruce

Notice how much writing I do explaining my position. Now read on to see what kind of response I get. Is there Scripture references? No. Does he answer my questions? No. He just comes up with more of his dogma, unsupported by even a phrase of Scripture. He also starts in on the name-calling. Classic Nicolaitan responses. Anyway, watch what happens next.

On 9/4/2018 12:05 PM, Roger wrote:
Sir, you ignore that the 'Law' is dead. Jesus said so. Any argument to the contrary is foolishness.
Your comment on sacrifices is putting words in my mouth I never said. I stated animal sacrifice only covered sin. Jesus' sacrifice eliminates the sin so NO MORE SACRIFICES ARE NEEDED. We are NOT to sacrifice animals anymore because if we do then we are saying the blood of Jesus wasn't enough. Dumb!

The Words of Jesus overrides anything in the OT. His covenant is what we are involved in. All of the rituals of the OT have been set aside, sacrifice is #1. Tithing is important as is an act of obedience and faith which is something that 'came through the cross'.

You can look at it any way you want. You can live under half the new covenant and half under the law, it's your choice.

Roger

He thinks I put words in his mouth, when he is the one who said that animal sacrifices were discontinued because of the sacrifice of Jesus. See the logical equivalent? If the sacrifice of Jesus eliminates animal sacrifices, doesn't that make animal sacrifices at least partly equivalent to the cross? In other words if "no more sacrifices are needed," then they must have been "needed" before the cross in some way that the cross now satisfies. If animal sacrifices don't relate at all to the cross, then they can continue. There might be other reasons for animal sacrifices then.

> Fools mock at the guilt offering, but the upright enjoy acceptance. (Proverbs 14:9, ESV)

He says, "The words of Jesus override anything in the Old Testament." Really? Where does it say that, anywhere? If He did say it, then that would be a good reason to crucify Him. In that case He would be breaking that which according to God cannot be broken. The reason He didn't say that is because He didn't override any Word of God in the Old Testament, especially the covenant. Roger doesn't have a single reference. Just more dogma. He has to use dogma because he doesn't have anything else. This is how Nicolaitans teach. "Don't listen to the Word of God, listen to me."

Subject: Re: Comments on your article Children Suffer Under a Silent Church, Part 1
From: Bruce Bertram
Date: Tue, September 04, 2018 4:14 pm
To: Roger
My apologies. I saw the "building the truth" and thought you might be doing that. You are correct that I can live as I wish. I prefer to live the whole of the Word and the New Covenant Law written on my heart of flesh, rather than some chopped up mess that produces what we see in the Church today.

I see now why you push the tithe so much. You are a pastor and you need it to make a living. I get it. And if you stop teaching what people want to hear such as the easy-believism of a Christ that gave us the Law then said, "Never mind" then you will lose your job. He kicked Israel out of the land for disobedience, but the Church can do what it wants? I don't think so. "The Word of the Lord endures forever."

I ignore that "the Law is dead" because Christ never said it and you are a liar for preaching it. The sacrifice of Jesus paid for our sins but you still can't answer Ezekiel 40-47. The blood of the sacrifices was not the same as the blood of the Christ. A sacrifice made with bloody hands never counted, and those who dumb down the Word by arbitrarily saying that some of it was eliminated make the blood of the Christ valueless. You, sir, are the one who is causing the abuse of children by refusal to teach the Word.

The words of Jesus ARE the words of the Old Testament (which designation was made by man) and nothing has been overridden by Him. It has only been obscured, twisted and nullified by the foolishness of self-anointed Church Nicolaitans taking it apart slowly but surely. The

so-called New Testament wasn't even assembled until about 200 A.D.
My, I guess "the Church" must've lived on nothing for all that time, huh?

Anyway, sorry for taking your time.
Shalom
Bruce

On 9/4/2018 6:14 PM, Rogerwrote:
Sir, Jesus said He came to fulfill the law. That means it is dead. As I
also said that there were things that came through the cross tithing being
one of them, sacrifice of animals was NOT one of them. Paul said we
have a new covenant and that means the old one is no longer in effect.
It's not rocket science. An elementary student can understand that. We
will agree to disagree.

Roger

Subject: Re: Comments on your article Children Suffer Under a Silent
Church, Part 1
From: Bruce Bertram
Date: Wed, September 19, 2018 10:43 am
To: Roger
Apparently, then, you are not even an elementary student.

For if you believed Moses, you would believe me; for he wrote of me.
But if you do not believe his writings, how will you believe my words?"
(John 5:46–47, ESV)

And also apparently, you do not believe the Bible. Paul connects the
"new covenant" with the same new covenant that Jeremiah spoke about.
If Paul is the writer of Hebrews 8 then he is saying that the "new
covenant" is with the house of Israel (where is the fictitious Church?)
and is God's Laws on the heart.

Now you know why the children are abused and the Church is silent.
You don't teach the Word and you don't follow the Word.

"You stiff-necked people, uncircumcised in heart and ears, you always
resist the Holy Spirit. As your fathers did, so do you. Which of the
prophets did your fathers not persecute? And they killed those who
announced beforehand the coming of the Righteous One, whom you

have now betrayed and murdered, you who received the law as delivered by angels and did not keep it." (Acts 7:51–53, ESV)

Shalom, Bruce

On 9/19/2018 11:17 AM, Roger wrote:
I hope you're not comparing yourself to Moses because your understanding of scripture lacks intelligence as well as facts. Paul's reference to the new covenant is the new covenant established by Jesus and included the Gentiles. That's who Pual was called to preach to. Remember the revelation Peter got with Cornelius? There's the Church.

There is no refuting this except for either stupidity or a complete refusal to believe scripture. Jesus Himself stated He was establishing the new covenant. I guess we will have to agree to disagree.

I really dislike the "agree to disagree" thing. I know it is intended to politely say "don't confuse me with facts, my mind is made up" but it also makes it seem as if the person is being reasonable when they are in fact obstinate, stubborn and refusing to consider opposing arguments. If we were talking about the best way to mow my yard, this would be fine. But since we are talking about the Bible, and a leader's teachings that are supposed to be based on it, the conversation is much more important and demands a better response.

He says I'm comparing myself to Moses? I wasn't the one who said to believe Moses is to believe Jesus, Jesus did. Either the guy is deliberately pretending to misunderstand or he's dumb on purpose. I think Jesus is fine with comparing Himself to Moses, but that isn't the point. The very clear, plainly stated point is that if one does not believe the writings of Moses one will not believe the words of Jesus.

Subject: Re: Comments on your article Children Suffer Under a Silent Church, Part 1
From: Bruce Bertram
Date: Wed, September 19, 2018 8:18 pm
To: Roger

I may have to stop the email exchange, but not because we agree to disagree. It is because you are not reading, using or following Scripture, and I can't make willingly blind people see.

Speaking of Paul:
For neither circumcision counts for anything nor uncircumcision, but keeping the commandments of God. (1 Corinthians 7:19, ESV)

I'm not comparing myself to Moses. Jesus said that if you don't believe Moses, you don't believe the words of Jesus either. How did you phrase it? Dumb.

The revelation Peter got for Cornelius was interpreted for us by, um, Peter.
So Peter opened his mouth and said: "Truly I understand that God shows no partiality, but in every nation anyone who fears him and does what is right is acceptable to him. (Acts 10:34–35, ESV)

See? If you actually read the Word, you can easily find out what God is saying. Peter didn't say a word about changing the Law, or eating a ham sandwich. Your interpretation isn't an interpretation, but a repetition of extra-biblical Church dogma.

Jesus did indeed speak of the new covenant. The very same new covenant given to Jeremiah, not some imaginary "Church" new covenant. Jesus said "This cup that is poured out for you is the new covenant in my blood." He didn't explain what He meant because everyone knew. The new covenant had been spoken of for at least 600 years before the incarnation. A plain reading of the Word (I know this is foreign to you) shows that the New Covenant is the Law written on a new heart of flesh. Talk about dumb on your part. "But behold, the hand of him who betrays me is with me on the table."

See, this is what Nicolaitans like you want. Twist the Word to say something it doesn't, destroy the plain meaning, and make it to where people have to go to you for the interpretation. You travel over land and sea to make a proselyte, then make him twice as much a son of hell as yourself.

Woe to you, scribes and Pharisees, hypocrites! For you travel across sea and land to make a single proselyte, and when he becomes a proselyte, you make him twice as much a child of hell as yourselves. (Matthew

23:15, ESV)

We can't figure the Bible out on our own according to you. You arbitrarily dismiss the Law so you won't have an objective standard to be judged by (at least in this life). The "tithe" (a ceremonial law according to Church teaching) which never was a tenth of the paycheck mysteriously passes the cross, but nothing else of the Law does. How strange is that? You have no Scripture support; you just make it up. So Nicolaitans rape kids and say they "love" them, using the very same cherry-picking doctrines you espouse. You deny the plain teaching of the Word and block me and many others from gaining the blessings from a whole Bible lifestyle and discipleship method. I notice in your articles and in your responses to me that you do not quote Scripture, just your Church dogma (except for a few verses quoted out of context, like that of Acts 10). What a surprise.

Your leadership, leading away from God's Word, is one of the main causes of child abuse and a silent Church. You shut the kingdom of heaven in people's faces and neither enter yourself nor allow those who would enter to go in. You are silent when it comes to Scripture, so you are reaping the fullness of your godless doctrine. We can agree to disagree, because I agree with Scripture and you do not. I wouldn't brag about that if I were you. Remember the millstone effect. Six times in the letters to the seven congregations Jesus commands them to repent. Repent therefore and bear fruit in keeping with repentance.

Shalom, Bruce

Read carefully and you'll see that Roger doesn't even realize he is now teaching two new covenants; one for Israel and one for the Church. How many do we see in Scripture? Only one new covenant.

And we'll let Roger have the final word in the exchange, though he just keeps repeating himself and as a former pastor of a Church is, not surprisingly, extremely light on answering with the Word of God.

On 9/19/2018 10:25 PM, Roger wrote:
I will say only one thing, Jesus established the new covenant. Nothing having to do with Jeremiah. The new covenant was with His blood and

His body. Remember the last supper? That's where He declared it. He fulfilled the old covenant, His words not mine. Done.
You may answer but I will not answer or read it. You have shown a total inability to understand or believe the Word of God.

Notice that Roger has no support from the Word for his contention that Jesus established the new covenant and "nothing having to do with Jeremiah." If that is true, then where is his other Bible reference? He doesn't have one; he just pulls it out of the air. Roger has the sort of dead reasoning earning the accusation from outsiders that the Church's faith is blind. If we just read the Word, it is plain that the new covenant Jesus inaugurated is indeed the same one that Jeremiah and Ezekiel wrote about 600 years before the Incarnation. And "fulfill" means to confirm or establish. So by Roger's own (blind) words Jesus confirms the old covenant. But if we question the Nicolaitan, he just wants us to trust that what the Bible says is not really what it says. We must blindly trust him to get the real interpretation, so authority is transferred from the Word to the Nicolaitan. See how that works?

Exchanges like this are extremely aggravating. Roger introduces an issue of silence from the Church in the face of child abuse, and then proceeds to illustrate the reason for the problem with his own teachings. Attempts to clear up his eyesight or hearing with real biblical solutions go unheeded. There is a real problem with child abuse and other immorality in the Church. The cause is the sort of scrambled, shallow and disconnected Bible teaching Roger and other Nicolaitans exhibit. They rip out the heart of God's New Covenant and substitute an artificial one made up of parts from a philosophical junkyard, then rail against the effects of their own Frankenstein construct. They advertise life to starving people; they deliver sawdust and sand.

Nicolaitans love the "agree to disagree" sort of closing argument. "Don't confuse me with facts, my mind is made up" and then shut down the conversation. He, like so many other

Nicolaitans, wants to trumpet his beliefs without any questioning. You have to take them at their word that whatever they are saying is the truth. No wonder people have so many intellectual problems with the Church's doctrine. Pharisees were famous for the same lack of intellect. The funny thing is that modern Nicolaitans cannot or will not make the connection that they are, actually, Pharisees.

I often think the following verse has a number of applications.

John 15:13, AV. Greater love hath no man than this, that a man lay down his life for his friends.

It applies to Jesus and His crucifixion first. He laid His life down and took it up again. It also applies to how we, in turn, give up our lives for Him. He showed us His enduring, boundless and eternal love at the cross; we show ours every minute of the day by living His Word. "Do we then overthrow the law by this faith? On the contrary, we uphold the Law" (Romans 3:31).We lay down our lives for our Friend and choose His way of living over our own understanding. His Law is not a law like man's laws when written on a heart of flesh and obeyed in love.

Thank you for reading. I hope you find freedom, maturity, fruit of the Spirit and abundant life in embracing all of the Word. Shalom.